THE 6

SECRETS TO

An Amazing Life

Transforming Mind, Body and Spirit

Maureen Kitchur, M.S.W., R.S.W.

Printed in Canada, by Blitzprint, Calgary AB   March 2010
2nd Printing, July 2010

Library and Archives Canada Cataloguing in Publication

Kitchur, Maureen, 1955-
     The 6 quantum secrets to an amazing life : transforming mind, body and spirit / Maureen Kitchur.
Includes index.
ISBN 978-0-9865754-0-2
     1. Mind and body therapies. 2. Meditation--Therapeutic use.
3. Self-actualization (Psychology). I. Title. II. Title: Six quantum secrets to an amazing life.

RC489.M53K55 2010   615.8'51   C2010-901954-7

Maureen Kitchur Consulting Inc.
1305 7th Street S.W.,
Calgary, Alberta, Canada, T2R 1A5
Website: www.kitchur.com
Email: maureen @kitchur.com

Acknowledgements

I practiced the 6 Quantum Secrets to An Amazing Life, and here's who showed up:

- Tracy Marsden, BSc., BSc. Pharm., wise friend, literary mentor, natural medicine consultant, incisive editor. Everyone should be lucky enough to have a friend like Tracy.

- Dr. George Gillson, medical and bio-identical hormone consultant, offering brilliant perspective and inspiration on the therapeutic application of hormones

- Theresa Queen, young message bearer of old wisdom

- Linda Sharp of Vancouver, gifted artist and designer of my cover

- Kerry Worth and Joel Pittet, cyber geniuses

- Bud Moore and Shelanda Kujala, patient photographers with great visual eyes

- And of course, my dear clients who indirectly and directly contributed to this book, and who continue to be my greatest teachers.

Contents

Chapter Two ~ WHY CAN'T I JUST GET OVER IT?

Chapter Three ~ I'M AT WAR WITH MYSELF!

Chapter Four ~ AM I ALL ALONE IN THIS?

Appendix ~ RESOURCES and LINKS

THE BEGINNING...

WE APPROACHED THE Great Pyramid of Giza in darkness, hours before sunrise, its massive shape looming over us, lit by the scant light of a new moon. Quietly, our small party ascended the heavy limestone slabs aligned along the base of the ancient pyramid, making our way toward the dim light emanating from the entryway. At a distance, guards patrolled the perimeter of the shadowed pyramid plain. There was silence. Giza and Cairo slept.

We stood before the only remaining Wonder of the Ancient World, electric with anticipation, our breath suspended. Our small party had obtained the remarkable privilege of hours of unrestricted access to the interior of one of the Seven Wonders of the World, and the only condition was that we visit it before daylight. And so the dim light beckoned us in, and our journey into the mystery began.

Hunched over, crouching, we crept into the narrow passage that descended from the opening. Ancient dust stirred beneath our feet, time-worn stone walls pressed in on us. Eighteen meters ahead, a choice presented itself: clamber up a steep incline which would usher us into a broader passageway and on into the King's Chamber, or descend into the bowels of the dark airless pyramid, 27.5 meters below ground, to the mysterious underground chamber rough-hewn out of rock, buried underneath 5.9 million tonnes of stone. Had we known how narrow was the passage into the underground chamber, how many of us would have chosen the lower path?

But as in life, no one knew precisely what lay ahead, and so we forged ahead, each choosing our own path. And each path yielded unique rewards — above us, the dark red granite walls of the King's chamber, with the mysterious sarcophagus housed within — too large to have fit through the passageway leading to the chamber. Below the King's chamber, in the belly of the pyramid, lay the small Queen's Chamber –its purpose unknown. And below the surface lay the dim underground chamber with its rocky interior, our photographs of it later turning out to be filled with orbs of light.

It is easy to lose track of time in the Great Pyramid; without a watch there are no clues to the passage of the hours or days. We had time to sit quietly, to meditate and reflect, to rest from the arduous climb. And so, hours later, when we made our way back out the passageway, first on our bellies, and then on our weary legs, we were delighted to be greeted by a rising sun and the dawn of a new day.

And in the few years that have passed since that experience, I've had a chance to think about its meaning. I am a therapist, a healer, and I've spent a number of years of my life living through the grit of my own experience, helping others to heal from theirs. More recently, I've learned and begun to teach about the quantum universe in which we are placed. I'm someone who has learned the value of finding the link between the small, local pain or experience and the larger context, the larger meaning of it. I seek to help my clients heal their suffering, to make sense of their lives, both within the small graces of everyday living, and at the metaphysical level where our existence is linked to the larger mysteries of the quantum field.

So while it is intriguing to ponder the many mysteries enfolded in the Great Pyramid, I am most interested in it as an easily understood metaphor for our experience. And it is the *structure* of the Great Pyramid that for me offers the richest parallel to our lives. This book, as you know from the title is about building a better life, and like the Great Pyramid, I want to help you design a life that will be strong and beautiful, with a structure that will support you, and an energy that will inspire those around you. This book is about healing the foundation of your life, and equipping you to scale the heights of your experience. It is about helping you to be practical, concrete, solid, able to withstand the storms, able to lean into the challenges of going deep within, and yet to rise up to an apex, to a beautiful peak, and in your own way to reflect the light of the world around you.

This book will help you to understand what being stuck is all about, and what to do when the underpinnings of your life no longer support or uphold you. It will introduce you to the Four Domains of Healing, where you can gain access to heal the structure of your life. It will offer you tools and knowledge to strengthen the foundation of your Brain and Body, strategies to heal the layers of personal History and self-talk that can weaken your structure, and processes to climb to new heights beyond your imaginings. It will introduce you, in user-friendly language, to concepts from the quantum universe, concepts and strategies that will teach you how to transform your life. So let's begin...

Introduction

HELP! I'M STUCK!

IF YOU'VE PICKED up this book, you or someone you know may need transformation. You may have become disconnected from your sense of personal power and feel unable to live your dreams. You may be struggling to figure out how to ramp up to a more inspired life. When this happens, it's often because brain and body, mind and spirit aren't working in synchrony.

I call this "being stuck." It can happen to anyone, and it can be an uncomfortable place to be, or just a flat and empty place to be. We can be stuck in one particular way, or we can be stuck in a whole bunch of ways — immersed in loneliness, anger, sadness, spiritual emptiness, hopelessness, addiction, shame, low self-worth, or any combination of these. Sometimes we just lack direction, feel bored or unfulfilled, or believe that we're not achieving our potential or living our purpose. It's often made worse by financial stress, so in tough economic times it can feel worse.

When we're stuck, we've usually *tried* lots of ways out, from friends to self-help to professional help to spiritual solutions, only to slide back into the pit (or the swamp, or the desert, or the dark night of the soul, or the void, or the boredom– you've got your own name for it.) And most people beat themselves up for sliding back, making that "stuck" feeling worse. People often feel embarrassed or apologetic when they can't seem to get on track, boost their feelings, move forward or "get over it," especially when they've done the best they can. And many people feel defective, like a failure, when they seem to be the only ones who can't get the Law of Attraction, the Twelve Steps, or well-respected self-help strategies to work for them. They can feel worse if they've also prayed for help and don't feel like they've received answers.

There's an ancient Greek myth about a guy named Sisyphus, who kept rolling a stone uphill, only to have it roll back down again and again. He spent all his time and energy rolling that stone upwards, and then watching his efforts wasted as the stone reversed course. A lot of people have reached exhaustion from trying to push themselves or their problem uphill, and they end up feeling defeated like Sisyphus, yet doomed to keep trying.

I want to tell you that regardless of whether a person has been stalled a *short time* or a long time, whether they cycle in and out of it, whether they can trace it back to childhood or not, whether it's the outcome of some recent setback or tragedy, and regardless of what efforts they've made to rise above it — *pain is pain*. And that pain is useful to us, because it's the mind-body's way of asserting that something needs fixing.

The fact is, there's a reason we haven't been able to break the cycle. *That reason is that our healing strategy or our life plan has a piece or two missing.* And if pieces are missing, the healing or dreams won't "take." You can renovate a house beautifully, but if the plumbing doesn't work, the house will never be functional or comfortable. You can restore a vehicle, but if a fan-belt or piston is missing, it won't run or get you anywhere. Human beings are just like that. If our strategy overlooks even one key part of what gets and keeps people happy, our efforts will fail.

So you need a strategy that encompasses all the parts of you, a strategy that will help you create a fabulous life that holds together. This book is intended to teach you that strategy, that blueprint for transforming your life. Here's what you'll learn: I'll teach you the amazing Six Quantum

Secrets that I use in my own life and that my clients have used with astonishing results. I will share with you amazing information about our actual physical and energy connection to the Universe, and how it is the link to produce the life of our dreams. Using secrets and strategies I have learned after more than 20 years as a psychotherapist and as a spiritual journeyer, I'm going to give you a comprehensive set of strategies to get you going and keep you out of the pit. I'll help you "upgrade" your energy and change the way the world responds to you. I'll give you empowering steps to really fix what's sabotaging your success, and to have well-earned happiness. I'll teach you to live your dreams!

But first I'm going to reveal to you powerful hidden blocks that get in the way of transformation. I want you to know about some of the most important ways your brain and body affect your happiness, and how your brain and body can block your spiritual and energy channels. Then I'll show you how to put that knowledge to work. I'll help you solve the sneaky, hidden, stubborn problems in your brain and body, your history and your self-talk that have quietly undermined you.

You see, in my years as a therapist, I've had a chance to really see what causes people to get stalled in life. I've treated all kinds of people in all kinds of adversity, average folks with average problems, and I've treated lots of people in extreme situations, including trauma survivors, people with extreme and complex mood disorders and personality disorders, and serious criminal offenders. My clients have included people born with advantages, and those without. They've included folks from spiritual backgrounds and those still searching for meaning, folks from all demographics, and of all ages — kids and teens and adults. I've learned what interfered with their happiness, and what got them unstuck.

Along the way I've also taught and consulted all over North America, and had the privilege of speaking in places ranging from church basements to the United Nations. And the people I've met in all of these settings have taught me to think outside the box, and to find the inner and outer resources and forces that create real happiness. I've learned that when we fix the hidden impediments or missing pieces that are messing up someone's strategy, it's easy to get connected to the quantum Universe, manifest surprising abundance, and live out one's deepest desires and purpose.

———— ⌣ ————

To get you on the path to transformation I want to introduce you to the Four Domains of Healing. These are the four areas of life which, when strengthened and healed *in an optimal order*, develop our readiness to effectively use *The 6 Quantum Secrets to Create an Amazing Life.*

The Four Domains are:

- Your Brain and Body
- Your History
- Your Inner Voice
- Your Connection to the Universe

Here's an overview of what we'll cover in the Four Domains as we move towards cleaning up your energy and helping you create the fabulous life you want:

Your Brain and Body: Your body and your brain are the hardware and software of the human computer. I'm going to give you some user-friendly information about some of the most common (but often hidden) things that get in the way of your brain doing its job naturally. I'll give you tips that will help you to overcome hardware problems, and strategies to get your brain working for you, instead of against you. If your biological self — your brain and body — is hosting an unresolved problem, fixing that can be *the* key to getting everything else working.

Your History: If your life experience has caused you to download some "junk," you won't run smoothly. So how do you know if your history is getting in the way? These days, it seems that more and more people describe themselves as having lived through tough childhoods, what with the increased prevalence of sexual abuse, domestic violence and addictions in families. Many people believe that "sucking it up," "putting it out of your mind," and getting over it are the best ways to move forward from childhood trauma, and there's a lot to be said for that. However, what if your history is actually affecting your biology and creating physical or emotional or spiritual "stuckness"? And if it is, how do you know whether you should go for counseling or therapy? And what kind of counseling or therapy? I want to help you be a smart consumer so that you know what to look for, what to ask for, and what to expect. (And what works!)

Your Inner Voice: Your self-talk can be loaded with viruses or annoying "pop-ups" that mess up your operation. If your biological self and/or your history got infected, chances are your inner self-talk has become full of defeat, pessimism and despair. I'm going to teach you my version of a simple "self-therapy" that you can do for this problem, whether you go for counseling or not. It's a strategy that gently (or firmly, if you need!) keeps you pointed in the right direction, and can help prevent *new* trouble from sticking to you. And it will make it easier to hear your deeper Inner Voice, which is a source of wisdom and higher guidance that will steer you accurately in the direction of your dreams when it's no longer overpowered by negative self-talk.

Your Connection to the Universe: Like a computer, we can only function for a short time on battery power. Eventually we need to be plugged in to a power source. So, when we're ready, we're going to take a look at the Big Picture — some amazing information about how the Universe can be enlisted to support you (in fact, it's already set up to serve you, but you may not have known how to get it "on your side.") You'll be able to make use of this information, because you won't have your brain and body sabotaging you, or your unhealed pain sucking you dry, and you'll already have the smart "self-therapy" daily tool to keep you afloat. You'll be able to focus and have fun with truly awesome metaphysical tools — the 6 Quantum Secrets to An Amazing Life — that will support you in creating a great life. And if a deep connection to God is one of the things you are seeking, you'll be much more able to experience that connection in a positive and uplifting way.

A WORD ABOUT THE "GOD" THING.

My own exploration of metaphysical and quantum tools and spiritual traditions has deepened a powerful sense of my connection to a larger Force. I've found that I'm as comfortable to call that force God as I am to call it the Universe. I experience that God force as expansive, as ecumenical, as open, and it therefore makes sense to me that that Force is well known in different cultures by different names. Regardless of how we name that Force, the energies connected to it are about abundance, and are incredibly powerful in creating the outcomes we desire. Working with those energies has created daily miracles in my life, and as I've taught these practices to my clients they too have experienced small and large miracles. I want to help you strengthen and heal the foundation of your life, so that you can use these tools to have your own miracles. Along the way, you may end up redefining your own view or paradigm of the Universe, and creating a new relationship to it.

Therefore, while this is not a religious book, I think you'll be surprised and delighted at how the powerful metaphysical processes in Chapter Four can awaken and deepen spiritual aspects of your being and your life. And at the same time, I think those tools and processes will raise your levels of discovery, fun and wonder, will help you live outside the box, and will also enable you to create the healthiest, most balanced, most expansive, and most exciting life you can have. Along the way to these outcomes, many people also find that an examination of their connection to the Universe leads them to their own personal sense of a God, a Higher Power or the divine.

I look forward to sharing the journey with you!

Now I'd like to introduce you to Julie Jones, a woman you're going to learn a lot about in this book. You'll learn about many of the questions we asked as she began her journey through the Four Domains of Healing, and you'll hear about the success strategies she employed as she learned to manifest her dreams. Julie, and other clients in this book, have kindly given permission for their stories to be told. They have chosen not to use their real names in this book, but are keen to have their stories of healing shared, in the intention that they will help others heal. In a couple of cases, for confidentiality and for teaching purposes, I have combined some elements of my clients' stories and presented them in a single composite story. Here's the beginning of Julie's true story:

Meet Julie Jones

Julie Jones felt completely "stuck" — she felt she couldn't move forward no matter how hard she tried. A smart, hardworking woman, she had struggled to put an unhappy childhood behind her, to put herself through graduate school, and to find some love and security. But when she called for an appointment, she choked back tears and described her sense of defeat, explaining that she was lonely, in financial trouble, employed in an unsupportive work environment, living in housing run by an unscrupulous landlord, and that none of the solutions she'd tried were helping her to feel any better or solve any problems. She'd budgeted, read good self-help books, practised the best self-care she could, but couldn't seem to come up with new results. Friendships weren't helping her growing sense of despair, and she was worried about burning her friends out. She didn't seem to have spiritual tools that worked, and previous therapy hadn't helped, so in desperation she'd gone to her doctor for an anti-depressant, but even medications didn't seem to be working.

"Is there a way out of this?" she asked. The answer was yes, and some of the reasons may surprise you.

My usual strategy with a new client is to review the four major domains of healing with them, as soon as possible. And so I began to explore the following questions with Julie:

Her Brain and Body: Were there any physical reasons for her sadness (including family heredity?) Were there any hidden health conditions that were keeping her off-balance? Why did several medications not work? Without addressing the biological factors potentially underlying Julie's sadness, all our other efforts to help her would have a hard time succeeding. I also knew that sometimes, solving the biological problems can mean getting completely unstuck without having to do other therapy.

Her History: Was she carrying any unresolved bad experiences at a cellular level? Unresolved trauma, including an unhappy childhood *can get stuck in your central nervous system!* and it can repeat the feelings over and over even though the events are long past. And it can do this, even if you've had talk therapy, even if you've used spiritual solutions, and even if you've used medication.

Her Inner Voice: Were there problems with Julie's inner narrative, her self-talk, her inner "script" that were creating a never-ending cycle of defeat? Our inner talk can get "anchored" in our brains, and it can take on a life of its own, and then undermine our other steps at problem-solving. And if our inner self-talk is despairing or resigned, it can make it difficult to hear our deeper Inner Voice, which is the source of wisdom and higher guidance which we all possess.

Her Connection to the Universe: Had she been spiritually trauma-tized? Did she believe in a negative God? Did she have experiences that cut her off from benefiting from positive energy in the Universe? Did she even know how to connect to that Force? We can know how to connect, but if other factors sabotage us, we can end up doubting or resenting that Force, and believing that we are out-of-favor and doomed to suffer.

I knew that when we had answered these inter-connected questions we would know exactly what to do to get her unstuck. *And I knew that there was an order in which we'd best address these issues, or our plan wouldn't work.*

I'll come back to Julie later, and tell you exactly how we addressed the missing pieces of her strategy and how she got unstuck. Then, you'll read about how Julie used the Six Quantum Secrets to an Amazing Life and really transformed her life! It's an exciting story, and it's full of strategies that will work just as well for you.

Chapter One

I'M STUCK! IS IT MY HARDWARE?

The First Domain of Healing:
Your Brain and Body

*"I sing the body electric ...
and if the body were not the soul, what is the soul?"*
Walt Whitman poet, humanist, free thinker

S OMEONE'S BRAIN LAY on the table. My scalpel hovered
over it. In a moment I would cut to the heart of this brain — its
limbic system — and peer into the tiny structures that had regulated the
emotional life of this brain's owner. Would the joys and sorrows of a
lifetime have left any traces? Would there be clues as to how healthy the
body was in which it had resided, or whether its owner had experienced
a traumatic history? Would I see the delicate pathways that had perhaps
sensed the mystical or divine?

My colleagues and I had come together at Marquette University to
discover more about the complexities of the human brain. From diverse
backgrounds, we each hoped to learn more about how this 3 lb. organ
could shape and power a human life. And so there in the lab, gloved and
gowned, we each beheld the brains before us in a different way — some

seeing it as an elegant computer, some as the housing of the personality, a few as the repository of the soul.

The human brain is wondrous to behold. A paradox, it is fleshy, wrinkly, deceptively humble looking, and yet the most elegant, complex computer of which we could ever conceive. At the same time, its all-powerful governance or dominion over the body is a myth, a half-truth. For at the front-end of life, the brain is only partly-developed, still wiring. At birth it has yet to receive some of its most critical programming — without which it will struggle to govern at all. And later, when the owner of a brain is old enough, it is the owner's choices in caring for his or her *body* that will ultimately determine the power or poverty of their brain. For only when the body is getting what it needs can the brain rise to its highest function — to map out a path to its owner's dreams.

So as my colleagues and I bent over the dissection table, those of us who were healers felt a particular gravitas, a sense of occasion. We were about to see for the first time the sensitive limbic area, an area profoundly shaped by the emotional and physical care it receives from birth onward, and which rewards its owner by sensing every joy and every heartache throughout a lifetime.

As we applied our scalpels, from underneath the layers of the thinking brain emerged the tiny, powerful emotional brain. In this chapter, I'll tell you about the most important parts of what we saw. I'll introduce you to some of the surprising things that happen in your emotional brain early in life, and I'll tell you about some of the powerful ways that your body influences your emotional brain. Later we'll look at how to combine this knowledge with healing, with your inner voice, and with a connection to the quantum universe to create the life you dream of.

———

Before we get to the surprises about your brain, here's something to consider: You have an electric body! Really. Ralph Waldo Emerson wasn't just being poetic when he talked about "the body electric." The fact is, you have a very powerful electromagnetic field in and all around your body. You have a powerful energy field capable of interacting with dynamic quantum energies contained in the physical universe. Your energy field helps to attract the life you dream about. But your Brain and Body must be in harmony in order to create that life. Your Brain and Body are not just an operating system, a container or a way to move around. Together they are meant to be a magnificent expression of You. But you must have a healthy connection between Brain and Body, a healthy energy field in order to show the world that beautiful You, and to attract the highest and best outcomes. So, if you're stuck, consider the following:

- **First, simply put, your brain and body must be working for you in some basic ways *or you will suffer and stay stuck.*** You can spend an entire life being distracted by Brain and Body problems and you can miss out on the whole reason you're here! We can do brilliant things to heal your history and help you hear your Inner Voice, but those results can be sabotaged if you aren't aware of some important things about your biological self. In some cases, life solutions are not possible at all before the brain and body are on an even keel. And even if you get some good help for some parts of your life, many smart solutions can be quickly undone by an out-of-control biology.

- **Second, your brain and body were the primary packaging for your "self" long before you ever developed a history in this life, or an Inner Voice to accompany you.** They accompany you throughout your life; they are yours to take care of. You may be a spiritual being having an earthly experience, but you're doing it in a body for a reason. So being wise about how our brains and bodies were meant to support us is essential. And it has been my experience as a psychotherapist (and as a woman!) that overcoming the ways our brains and bodies uniquely challenge us is often a big part of how our best learning is meant to occur.

- **Third, when the brain and body are not in harmony, they can create a huge impediment to making sense of the Universe or God or a higher power, and to being able to effectively pray, meditate, use focused intention or be mindful.** You see, because you, your brain and body are connected to the larger world around you and to the even larger Universe in which you find yourself, disruptions in your brain, body, history or self-talk can dramatically affect whether the Universe seems to work for you or against you. Brain and body conditions that fly under the radar can seriously mess up what your personal energy creates for you, and can be a major cause for being stuck. A brain and body out of harmony can prevent us from being able to access those larger *meta*physical resources (*meta* means "beyond," so we're talking about those forces and resources that are beyond what you can perceive through your five senses alone.) Some people do connect to the divine when their brain and body are not in harmony: people with life-altering chronic illnesses sometimes find that their illness fosters their spirituality. In other words, a broken body can be the path to spiritual awareness, but for most of us the path of divine suffering is a difficult one, and I want to help you find easier ways.

QUANTUM SURPRISES ABOUT YOUR BRAIN AND BODY

Since you're going to see the word "quantum" more than a few times in this book, let's get clear about what people mean when they use the word. You've probably understood it to mean a major breakthrough or a sudden advance, like when someone refers to "a quantum leap" in thinking or design. Well, the reason people describe a sudden, logic-defying advance as "quantum" is this: In the simplest terms, a quantum is something so small that it can't be divided.

And not too long ago, scientists discovered that this smallest indivisible bit of energy in the universe can, in a logic-defying way, be two things at once: a particle and a wave, and it can apparently be in two places at once! This quantum particle can instantaneously communicate with itself when it is in two different places. This instantaneous "leap" is a "quantum leap," and as you'll see, it tells us something pretty amazing about the universe. It means that energy and molecules within the universe are connected in "quantum" ways that defy logic. So things you may have thought were unconnected can in fact influence each other hugely! Very powerful things are possible because of the invisible, instantaneous inter-connectedness of all things. This book will teach you about some of the ways that *you* and the physical universe are inter-connected, how you influence each other, and how to awaken and use that influence to produce great outcomes and the kind of life you've been dreaming about.

So let's start with some quantum surprises about your Brain and Body: **You have an energy field.** *And what you put into you, your experiences, your self-talk, and how you take care of yourself all affect the kind of energy you will give off.* And more than that, they affect the kind of energy *you attract back to you.* If what goes into you and what goes on inside you is positive, you'll create a powerfully positive energy field that will attract back to you more of that kind of energy. The more you know about how to create a positive energy field for yourself, the more you will create and influence the outcomes in your life. By the same token, if there are disturbances in your brain and body, your energy field may be powerfully inhibiting the kind of life you want. Messed-up energy can create a kind of energetic "holding pattern" which can have you circling around, unable to break free.

You see, your Brain and Body are constantly sending out messages to the world you live in, and to the Universe that surrounds you. This can be an incredible source of power if your brain and body are working well, or it can be why you're living a nightmare. Since a lot of people don't know *how* this process occurs, here's a bit more user-friendly science to explain your connection to the Universe:

First of all, as material beings with personal boundaries, we tend to think that we are separate from one another, and that if there is a God or a Source of creative intelligence that we are also somewhat separate or distinct from that God or Source. Interestingly, science has something different to tell us. We have long known that we are molecular beings—literally, since we are made of molecules. In fact, our molecules are composed of energy temporarily slowed down enough to take the form of "you" or "me," and so each one of us is really just energy manifested as grouping of molecules. We are surrounded by a sea of other molecular groupings—all other matter and life forms around us are formed of energy slowed down into molecular form.

So we are all part of a vast molecular soup, which is the Universe. And we're not only in the soup, we *are* the soup! This means that we are not actually separate at all from everything else in the Universe—we have just had the illusion of being so.

And to take it a step further, we might say that when it comes to the Universe, we are like a chip off the Big Block. That's because we are a holographic piece of the Universe—a piece of a holograph has embedded in it *all* of the information of the larger whole from which it is derived. Just as a stem cell is a microcosm containing all the same basic life information as the human body, we humans are a microcosm containing in smaller form all the same basic life information that is present in the Universe around us! This is part of what physicists mean when they refer to us being in a holographic universe.

Quantum physicists also speculate that since all forms of life are interconnected, we are naturally interconnected in a web of *communication* too, at levels that we may not consciously be aware of. It is known that particles of matter can influence one another instantaneously across vast distances, and it is thought that the so-called empty space or dark matter between things is a living part of the interconnectedness of all things. So particles that appear to be disconnected from one another are really not, and that's why they can instantaneously communicate. This connected, communicating relationship between apparently disconnected particles is a subatomic property referred to as "nonlocality" or "quantum entanglement." So we're not only in a molecular soup, but it's a thick soup!

Quantum physicists also tell us that we molecular beings are part of what is called the Field, an endless, timeless field of interconnected vibrating energy waves that spread out to infinity. This full name of this quantum field is the Zero Point Field, and it's called that because in temperatures of absolute zero—which is the lowest possible energy state—where all matter has been removed and there should be a true still vacuum, it turns out that energy fluctuations are still detectable! The quantum dance of energy just goes on and on!

And finally, as molecular beings we are not only composed of energy and linked to that larger Field of dancing energy, but we also have our *own* energy fields, and we emanate and receive energy. In fact, that is how we appear to be linked to the Field.

So we are a bundle of radiating energy and completely part of the sea of energy that is all around us. *In other words,* **you are in an energetic relationship to the world around you, and to the larger Universe as a whole.**

Your Brain and Body are at the centre of *your* Field, the medium through which you connect with everything around you. They help to shape the kind of energy you give off and so they help to shape your whole life. So let's go deeper now into the First Domain of Healing — Your Brain and Body. We'll look at some of the elementary but powerful ways that your Brain and Body can get off-track — the often hidden but very common factors that make it hard for people to feel good, think optimistically, plan, and even to pray, meditate or have any faith in spiritual solutions. I see these traps in people's lives every day and I want to help you declare war on them! After we look at how these traps show up, we'll talk about what we can do about these things. And don't worry, there's much we can do, because the Brain and Body remain "plastic" throughout life, which means they can respond well to many different kinds of corrective measures.

Your Happiness Thermostat and Your Early Wiring

You have a happiness thermostat. The temperature of your happiness gets set partly by your genes — heredity just sets some people up to be happier. Some scientists call this your happiness "set point." But there are other important influences over how happy you can be.

One big influence over your happiness occurs early in life — while you're still in the womb. When you're in utero, your mother's food choices, use of alcohol and drugs, and even her stress levels start wiring your brain. If your mother had a superb diet, meditated, and was happy and fulfilled, you're in luck! You were more likely to be a happy baby.

But regardless of genetics and early influences in utero, your brain and the happiness thermostat in your brain aren't even remotely "hardwired" by the time you are born. Certain childhood *experiences* will help to further set your thermostat. The reason for this is that your brain is incredibly "plastic" — experience can wire it and re-wire it throughout life!

As a matter of fact, we probably shouldn't even use the terms "hardware" or "hardwire" anymore, because research shows that the brain is a much more changeable organ throughout the life cycle than we ever knew before. We can use the newer term "firmware" and say that some of your most important firmware starts wiring right after birth. That's right, immediately after birth an amazing thing begins to happen. It turns out that the parts of your brain that will regulate your emotional life *start to wire themselves because of the type of relationship you have with your primary caregiver!* What happens is that as you are held and rocked, as you are attended to and loved, as you are fed and played with, and even (in fact especially) as your parent just gazes at you and smiles affectionately at you, *those experiences actually build brain structures!*

A TINY STRUCTURE WITH A BIG JOB

Think of a tiny sea-horse. The main brain structure that wires during this "bonding" or "attachment" process is a little sea-horse-shaped body right in the centre of the brain, called the hippocampus. It's part of the limbic system, and it plays an important role in your emotional brain. Once wired, it is involved in attention, emotion, fear, dreaming, learning and memory, to name just a few of its roles. Bonding and attachment in infancy and childhood are crucial to wire it to do its job well.

For those people who are fortunate to have good bonding experiences with a parent, the hippocampus is now firmwired to contribute to a happiness "set." The hippocampus and other parts of the emotional brain will now support you from childhood onward to tolerate frustration, cope with disappointment, soothe yourself in healthy ways, and make you less vulnerable to unmanageable bouts of anger, sadness and anxiety. As a matter of fact, research shows that you'll be less likely to struggle with addictions too. These things are not only good indicators of your happiness "set", but they are indicators of your ability to stay balanced: they mean you can "self-regulate."

When your emotional brain is optimally wired from the get-go, it is set up to produce and make good use of serotonin and dopamine, the main brain chemicals or neurotransmitters that operate in the emotional brain. And as a result, you'll be better-equipped to avoid certain forms of depression, anxiety, compulsive behaviors such as eating disorders, addictions to food, drugs, alcohol, sex, gambling, spending, and anger problems such as "limbic rage" (which is a feeling of primitive unmanageable anger.) As we'll talk about later, compromised wiring of the emotional brain is one of the reasons that mood-stabilizing drugs, including serotonin-boosters, are some of the most frequently-prescribed class of pharmaceuticals nowadays.

Something else about these early bonding experiences: individuals who didn't have the best early bonding and attachment are more likely to experience an on-going yearning for connectedness and belonging. They can be more sensitive to abandonment and rejection, and even *perceived* abandonment and rejection. They can experience loneliness. Some folks may find they fear being alone, so they get needy or clingy, and this can compromise the way they do relationships. And therefore, they often make poor choices and decisions about relationships, because they need to just fill the void.

Not having the best attachment and bonding experience leaves your brain a little less able to handle stressors, you end up not coping so well sometimes, and you start having experiences of getting in trouble, getting blamed or rejected, and you start to *believe* that that's the way it will always be. From there on in, it's *you* creating your reality: you start to *feel* powerless in relationships and social situations, you start to *expect* trouble, and you start to live out your own predictions. Fortunately there are great antidotes to this problem. We really are very powerful people, and in Chapter Three we'll take a look at how we can change the script and live out a very different reality.

By the way, while we're on the subject of attachment, bonding and abandonment, I want to tell you about something I've seen over and over in the lives of my clients. The experience we have of our first care-givers creates an internal "model" in us, and it shapes how we relate in all relationships, but especially our relationship with God or a Higher Power. If our early experiences of "authority" figures are of them being judging or abandoning or critical or only able to give conditional love, then we tend to project that model on to our sense of who or what God is. Another way of saying it is that those are the "lenses" through which we see the Universe, and it's not a pretty picture.

So we have the irony that while we're walking around with pain and hurt from our experiences in our families and *most* need a connection to, or help from, a compassionate loving higher power, we often are the *least* likely to be able to experience that! Said another way, the world-view a child is exposed to can limit their ability to see the Universe as the expansive, abundant place it really is. Fortunately, as you'll see in later chapters we have good ways to heal these experiences and free you up to find out other things about God and the Universe, including some of the amazing power you can exercise.

As you're reading this, you might feel tempted to be angry at your parents if they didn't give you a great bonding experience, and thus the best "wiring." Although this is often a legitimate source of pain, the truth is that most parents do the best they can with what they've got. Parents who provide less-than-optimal parenting (or downright terrible parenting) usually didn't have better themselves, so they often lack the awareness or skills to correct the "model" they learned. In Chapter Two, we'll talk about what to do if your childhood experience wasn't so great. There are smart ways to bring healing to those experiences, to process your very legitimate sadness, disappointment and anger, while *not* getting caught in blaming and staying stuck in the past.

Speaking of your brain and God, I want to tell you something even more amazing about the powerful area of your brain that regulates your emotional life. Not only is your limbic system deeply involved in your happiness "set" and your ability to self-regulate, but it is believed by some scientists to be where your soul hangs out! Scientists now know that deep in the structures of this region of the brain lies an important part of our capacity for spiritual experience. Together, limbic structures and the temporal lobe enable human beings to have religious, spiritual and mystical experiences! (The actual limbic structures involved are the hippocampus, which we've already talked about, and its neighbor the amygdala, a tiny little almond-shaped body right next door. They're both deep in the centre of the brain.) So for healthy spiritual experiences, we rely on this part of the brain to be working normally.

Solving Brain and Body Challenges

Is it Your Genes, Your Diet or Your Hormones?

So now you have some sense of how the firmwiring from early bonding and attachment can affect your "happiness thermostat," your relationship style and your experience of God or the Universe. And there are a few other ways that experience and your brain can shape each other, mess up your energy and interfere with your happiness. Your genes, your diet and your hormones can all play a role, too! Fortunately, there are good antidotes to these problems, but only if you know enough to spot the problems in the first place!

Notice that I said "experience and your brain can shape each other." That's right — it's often a chicken-and-egg kind of thing. There are many problems and conditions that we are seeing that no one is exactly certain how much is heredity (including your family's genetic make-up) and how much is the result of certain bad experiences or environmental conditions. For example, research suggests that there are likely some genetic factors at work in addictions, learning problems, Attention Deficit Disorder (ADD) and its cousin Attention Deficit Hyperactive Disorder (ADHD), anxiety, and certain forms of depression. However, not everyone in a family with those histories ends up with those conditions. And even one identical twin can develop a disorder that doesn't show up in their twin.

> Why doesn't everyone in a family develop the conditions that they are carrying a gene for? Well, one of the things we know is that genes have to be "turned on" like a switch in order to shape the life of an organism. And it turns out that certain types of experiences trigger genes to "turn on" (it's called "transcription") and only then can they run their programs in people. As a matter of fact, there's a whole branch of genetic science called "epigenetics" which explores how the genes we inherit from our parents are altered and turned on and off by exposure and experiences throughout life.

Back to the "chicken-and-egg" conditions in which we can't precisely tell whether the origins are genetic or experiential or both. A lot of these conditions can be extremely powerful and yet can slip past detection by you and even your professional helpers for surprisingly long periods (like decades!) They can create devastating effects in your life until someone recognizes them and knows what to do about them.

And when something like ADD is at play, it not only creates problems of its own, but also gets in the way of resolving other challenges. The good news is that we don't have to know whether in fact it's genetic or environmental — we just have to be observant enough to detect that it's operating, and then there's a whole range of solutions we can apply. And let's be clear: if conditions are operating unchecked or undetected, or known but unmanaged, *they will keep you stuck.* These conditions must not be left flying under your radar, because that is exactly when you'll find yourself stuck, sending out negative energy, self-sabotaging or hopeless. Take Laura for example:

Hidden Attention Deficit Disorder: Laura's Story

Laura was a 39 year old professional, with lots of good things in her life — loving husband and kids, interesting work, close friends, strong values. But inside, she was desperately unhappy, felt a great emptiness, and a constant sense of being overwhelmed. She found herself with a frequent impulse to take on new projects, and was fearful about the financial liabilities and shortage of time that she had created for herself. She was able to concentrate, but more so on the things she loved, and even that would create problems for her by distracting her from other responsibilities. Laura also had had a long struggle with her weight, and with its elevating effects on her blood pressure. Her husband was frustrated, she felt confused by her own repeating cycle of behavior, and both of them were concerned about Laura's increasing tendency to use alcohol to relax and put it all aside temporarily.

Of course we looked at all the standard things that therapists look at: family history, childhood trauma, Laura's self-talk, and the marital relationship. And no question, there was important healing to do in each of those areas. But a solution to Laura's stuckness would not be reliable and lasting unless it included a long hard look at her biology. And sure, we looked at nutrition and fitness, but there was a clue when Laura couldn't seem to stick to any of her resolutions or even behavioral contracts in these areas. For it was as we looked at the overall pattern of what *didn't* work that we found the key to her stuckness: one day I said to this bright, competent, educated, loving, hardworking woman, "Laura, I think you've got Attention Deficit Disorder." And then Laura's life was able to change.

At first, she couldn't believe it. How could she have made it all the way through high school, university and professional school if she had ADD? After all, she had been courted by professional firms, held highly responsible positions, raised kids, run businesses. So when I told her I was certain she had ADD, she didn't really believe me, but she was polite about it. She went to see her doctor, who didn't believe me either. But what I knew was that in some adults, particularly if they went to school in an era when learning problems flew under the radar, and *particularly* if they were academically successful, ADD can go undiagnosed for decades!

And I had already looked closely at the other three Domains of Healing, and my gut and experience told me that unless we considered the possibilities in the biological realm — the Brain and Body — our other solutions wouldn't "take." It turns out, that had been the missing piece of Laura's life strategy for decades! Her doctor then sent her to a specialist for a third opinion, and sure enough, medication was recommended. Laura and her doctor were shocked to discover a short time later that her blood pressure came down, and a new sense of well-being emerged. Gone was the unhappiness, the scatter, the sense of pressure and failure. Laura experimented for a few months to get stabilized on the best medication regime. She found that one well-known medication caused her eye twitches, but did not disturb her sleep. She found that another medication was a bit more stimulating and couldn't be taken late in the day, but it didn't give her eye twitches. So she eventually settled on a regime that included the stimulating medication in the morning, and the non-stimulating one late in the day if she needed it.

Laura reported that as her meds stabilized her, she no longer procrastinated, she felt more comfortable to set boundaries and not rescue people at her own expense and time, and she was able to streamline areas of her work. She felt able to begin to clean up what she termed the "carnage," the disarray that she had created in her life before she was diagnosed. She also found she didn't worry so much what people thought of her anymore, and lost her initial sense of shame about her diagnosis. She also gained real perspective on her siblings, realizing that ADD was pervasive in her family, and so she prepared to "come out" so that they might have the benefit of her experience. (She would wait a while until she was sure they could see the changes in her, so that their own resistance to the information might be more easily overcome.) She also felt enlightened and therefore empowered to be able to watch out for ADD issues in her kids. Laura reported that while she still had a tendency to run late and do too much, she recognized that she was a working mother and was not alone in this tendency. Her diagnosis of ADD changed her life. Laura was unstuck and free to move ahead in her life, to keep her balance and priorities, and to be in possession of herself in a way that had never before been possible.

I see women like Laura almost every week in my practice. Often in their 30s and 40s, they are mystified about why they are so tired, scattered, overweight, depressed and hopeless. They are bright and caring people, and are all the more mystified about their own self-sabotaging behavior. And it isn't just 30 and 40 year old women who show up with these issues. ADD can hide out in a wide variety of people, creating chaos. In Laura's case, it wasn't exactly clear whether a specific environmental factor had turned on a gene to produce ADD in her, although it is sometimes more obvious in some people's lives. In fact, there are a couple of known environmental factors that can absolutely create the conditions for ADD or ADHD to thrive. Nutrition is one of those conditions:

WHICH FOODS AND HABITS HELP OR PREVENT ADD?

A lack of adequate protein and essential fatty acids can rob your brain of the raw ingredients it needs to produce dopamine, a brain chemical that operates in an area in the front of your brain — your Pre-Frontal Cortex. Dopamine acts like a conductor or a traffic cop to sort out the signals in your brain and help you concentrate, pay attention and learn. If you don't produce enough of it, your brain and behavior will be "scattered." That means you have to have adequate and *regular* protein intake every day in order for your brain to work properly. How much protein? Well, that varies according to whether you are sedentary, a body builder or a marathoner. There is no one agreed-upon guideline, but an average of the recommended Canadian and American guidelines for protein intake is 1 gram for every 2 lbs. of body weight every day. (So an average 150 lb. person would need 75 grams of protein every day. That's about the equivalent of three cans of tuna, or three chicken breasts.) And we're talking healthy protein, not just fatty burgers and greasy takeout. So nuts, beans, fish, chicken and dairy or tofu (unless you're allergic to one of these) should be a part of your diet every day, and should be consumed approximately every four hours. That regularity of protein intake will also help to keep your blood sugar stable, which helps with mood control!

All of this means that you and your kids *have to have breakfast!* Protein and fruit shakes are a great, fast breakfast to ensure energy and concentration at work or school. You also need the fatty acid DHA, which is found in fish, to keep your brain working well, and you can get it in regular servings of fish and/or from fish oil capsules. There are even tasty fruit-flavored chews now that provide a daily dose of DHA. In the Appendix, I'll give you some links to check out if you want more information about protein guidelines, or if you need more sophisticated natural supplements or medication to address attentional issues.

We also know now that for every hour per day that a child watches TV, there is a 10% increased chance of them being diagnosed with ADD. A child who watches four or five hours of TV each day has a 40—50% chance of being diagnosed with ADD! Even video games are now thought by scientists to trigger brain changes which can cause learning or behavior problems in kids and adults. And we see a lot of ADD and ADHD in kids (and later in adults) who come from highly stressful environments, and/or who've experienced traumas in their families, because the brain's development and function is affected if it is exposed to chronic or severe stress.

So you can see that if you or your child happen to have a genetic predisposition to ADD or ADHD (i.e. if it runs in your family — *even if you don't know it!*) and if you have a highly stressful family environment and/or you spend lots of time in front of TV or video, *and* have a lousy diet, you've got a "hot" biological environment in which ADD or ADHD can easily show up!

And if this is going on it will be way easier to feel stuck, and to feel that you don't have the concentration or focus to know where to start to move yourself forward. The energy you send out will be "scrambled" and so will your results. This is why I get people to look at the First Domain of Healing — the Brain and Body — often before we even look at the other three Domains. If the missing piece of their strategy is found here, all the rest of our work is made faster and easier, and sometimes we don't have to do any other work at all! Take Joel, for example:

Mysterious Anxiety: Joel's Story

Joel was a really friendly, personable 24 year old man who worked for a paint supplier. He had a pretty solid relationship with his family, and also with his girlfriend of two years. He had no trauma history, and no spiritual struggles. But he had developed a problem in the First and Third Domains — his Brain and Body, and his Inner Voice. In the past six months, he had developed anxiety symptoms that wouldn't go away, and he had started to have an anxious "tape" that played in his head. It played more and more: as he was backing up and driving out of a parking lot, as he was hoisting paint cans, as he was going on his break with his co-workers (whom he really liked), and as he hung out with his girlfriend (whom he really, *really* liked!) And what he noticed was that had begun fearing his anxious feelings, and he was worried because he didn't know where they were coming from or how to get rid of them.

When I took Joel's history, I didn't see any obvious clues that his stuckness was coming from the second or fourth Domains (his history or his spiritual framework), and I knew that anxious self-talk was therefore likely related to his Brain and Body. There was no hereditary anxiety in his family that he knew of, and no depression either. (If we're looking at anxiety in the family history, we always look at depression too, since mood disorders often co-exist in the same family — one aunt or uncle might have had anxiety, and one grandparent or cousin on that same side of the family might have struggled with depression, for example.

Or one or more of them might have struggled with *both* anxiety and depression. If there was a history of one or more mood disorders on *both* sides of the family, Joel would be very vulnerable to a mood disorder.)

So, since there was no known history of a mood disorder in the family, Joel and I began to look at what had changed in his life around the time the anxiety came on six months earlier. It took a while to figure it out, but what had changed was his diet. Joel had started to work an earlier and longer shift, and he found it affected his appetite. He was a big, hungry guy, and he *loved* chicken and tuna. So he had started having two cans of tuna for breakfast, two at his mid-morning break, two chicken breasts for lunch, and usually two for supper. Joel was getting almost 200 grams of protein a day! That was more than twice the recommended intake for his body weight (using the protein guideline in the box on the previous page) and it was too much of a good thing. (It was boosting his dopamine in his pre-frontal cortex and driving down his serotonin in his limbic system, making alertness overpower his brain's calming function, so he was one agitated guy!)

Joel seemed a little dubious when I told him I wanted him to cut his protein in half and come back in a week. I suggested he fill in those missing calories with complex carbohydrates like whole grains, fruits and vegetables, and healthy fats like olive oil, served on salads or on some of the remaining tuna and chicken (which would be way easier on his kidneys, since too-high doses of protein are hard on kidneys.) Joel returned a week later, relaxed and amazed. The anxious talk in his brain had stopped, and he felt physically calm. He wanted some help to take a look at whether he was ready to commit to his girlfriend, and so we were easily able to address that issue, because biological agitation and anxiety were no longer in the way of him being able to think clearly about that large life-issue.

Joel is an exception when it comes to anxiety disorders. As I've suggested, a lot of people have anxiety disorders that are more related to family heredity and/or trauma. There are all kinds of anxiety disorders including panic, phobias, acute stress, obsessive-compulsive disorder, and even agoraphobia, which is anxiety about being in certain places (usually there's a fear of going out or being in public.) Some of these are more likely to start in childhood, and several are more prevalent in females than in males.

You may need some help from a therapist to sort out whether your anxiety can be addressed in the First Domain only (through biological solutions such as nutrition and medication and biofeedback), or whether your anxiety needs to be addressed in the Second and Third Domains, through healing your history and your self-talk. (To heal your history, there's a great method available called EMDR, which is short for Eye Movement Desensitization and Reprocessing. When used by a therapist who is well-trained in it, it does a remarkable job of healing the past. I'll tell you more about it in Chapter Two. And to heal your self-talk, there are a variety of strategies, one of which I'll teach you in Chapter Three.) Some people's anxiety needs healing in all three Domains, since their biology, personal history and inner talk are all part of the problem. And that's important to realize, since as I've told you, if even one key piece of your strategy is missing, you can stay stuck. So if you're having problems with anxiety, now you might have some clues about what areas of your life might hold the key to getting you unstuck.

Post-Traumatic Stress Disorder

"I can't sleep, I can't focus, I can't relax!" Sounds like anxiety, doesn't it? Or maybe anxiety with a little ADD mixed in? Maybe it's neither. Maybe it's Post-Traumatic Stress Disorder, which has anxiety associated with it, and which can also show up alongside or even masquerade as ADD. If undetected and untreated, it can cause people to be stuck for months or years or decades.

PTSD is short for Post Traumatic Stress Disorder, and it's a set of symptoms that can show up after an unresolved major trauma. You may have heard of it, and thought that only soldiers get it. It is true that it's very common in soldiers who've been in battle. In the Civil War it was called "soldier's heart," and in the First World War it was referred to as "shell shock" because it was thought to be caused by being exposed to the shelling that occurred in war. But the fact is, PTSD is also a fairly common after-effect for people who have experienced a shocking or traumatic event like physical or sexual abuse, exposure to family violence, serious car accidents, and natural disasters. Symptoms can include insomnia and nightmares, anxiety or panic, and difficulty concentrating (making it hard for some people to learn or remember as effectively as they used to.) It can also include flashbacks, and this is because unresolved trauma gets stuck in your central nervous system and can "repeat" like a broken record or a stuck CD, making you feel like the trauma is happening all over again. It can last for months or years or decades until it's properly diagnosed and treated, but in the meantime it can fly under the radar, looking like an anxiety disorder in some settings, or more like depression or a sleep disorder or ADD in other settings. When it flies under the radar, it can completely interfere with a person being able to get on successfully with life.

PTSD belongs in the First and Second Domains of Healing, because it is both an after-effect of traumatic personal experience *and* there is evidence that a hereditary component may make some people more susceptible to it. And we also know that if you have first-degree relatives with a history of depression (i.e. your parents or siblings), you can be more vulnerable to developing PTSD if you have a major or shocking trauma.

So if you are stuck and you have any of the brain and body symptoms listed in the paragraphs above, it may be that your biology, in combination with an unresolved trauma, is the cause. Fortunately, you don't need to know exactly what factors are "anchoring" PTSD. You just need to be aware that if you have symptoms of PTSD, it will be essential to get them healed in order to get unstuck. Therapists who are well-trained in EMDR (Eye Movement Desensitization and Reprocessing) will be able to help you resolve PTSD, usually completely. In Chapter Three I will tell you about some people who used EMDR to heal their experiences of major trauma (including a prison guard who was held hostage), and along with it, healed their physical symptoms and their self-talk, and who were then "unstuck" and able to really get on with life.

Depression

Another "chicken-and-egg" condition which we see more and more these days is depression. When I started my career as a psychotherapist over 20 years ago, it was rare to see children and teens showing up with depression that required medication, and we certainly didn't see the incidence of depression that we now see in adults either. Was it just because people didn't talk about it? It's doubtful.

Decades ago we had healthier nutrition, greater ties to our communities and families, less pollution in the environment, no synthetic hormones and "additives" floating around in our rivers and drinking water, less electronic interference in child development, and even a different sense of life not needing to be hurried, a slower pace in which people learned to wait for things, tolerate delay, not require "instant" solutions, all of which created a different environment for the brain and our biochemistry. Parallel to changes in all those elements in western society, we have seen dramatic increases in mood disorders.

GARBAGE IN, GARBAGE OUT.

There's a form of "garbage" that may be responsible for more of the widespread mood disorders we see today than almost anything else. Did you know that when certain forms of plastics degrade they form compounds known as "xenoestrogens?" "Xeno" means "stranger" or "foreign." If these foreign estrogens end up in our water or in contact with our foods or beverages, they enter our bodies.

All of us, male and female, have receptors on our cells that allow some cells to take in estrogen. These foreign estrogens fool our cells and attach to these receptor sites, and create estrogenic effects in our bodies (male or female!) That means women who may already have enough estrogen end up being way too estrogen-dominant (which means their progesterone isn't enough to compete and keep a proper balance.) So they can end up weepy, irritable, with mood-swings,

---

bloating, and poor sleep. These foreign estrogens create problems for males, too. Nature gave males a small amount of natural estrogen because that's all they need. But when extra estrogen is added into a male, it can mess up his total hormone balance. There is speculation that these foreign estrogens may be implicated in the very high number of boys that are now born with one or more undescended testicles, and in the changing ratio of female-to-male live births in areas of western world.

So pay attention to all the warnings you hear these days about plastic beverage containers, and avoid heating or microwaving your food in plastics that are not designed for that purpose. As it is, you are already getting xenoestrogens in water and through the food chain. Do everything you can to reduce your sources of them.

And there's no need to get fearful about this subject. Just be cautious, and make sure that you are eating a healthy, balanced diet with lots of filtered water, well-washed fruits and vegetables, whole grains, healthy proteins, and essential fatty acids like Omega 3's, and as few processed carbs and sugars as possible, so that your body has the raw materials it needs for good health and a happy immune system. This way, your body will produce fewer "free radicals" and it will use the anti-oxidants from healthy foods to fight whatever "free radicals" are floating around in your system. For a lot of people, these are the ways to prevent disease conditions, to help medications work if they are needed, and to prevent Brain and Body conditions from contributing to "stuckness."

Let's look more closely at how depression contributes to being stuck. First of all, depression can start inside you (that's called endogenous depression), or it can be triggered by outside conditions (that's called exogenous depression). Inside forms of depression can have hereditary roots, and/or can be triggered by disturbances in your biochemistry, including hormone imbalances, blood sugar instability and/or poor nutrition. Depressions that come from "outside" triggers such as a stressful or traumatic event like a loss can end up affecting your biochemistry, which can keep the depression going. (Chicken-and-egg again!) Whether the depression seems to stem more from inside conditions than outside conditions, there may be a genetic vulnerability underlying either form of depression. We are usually able to heal these forms of depression whether we know there are hereditary roots or not.

Sometimes depression is obvious, and sometimes it's hidden — from others, or even from yourself! Depression can rob you of energy, motivation, perspective, sleep, wakefulness, libido (your sex drive), and appetite (or appetite control.) In these situations, it is possible to *not* know that you have depression, and think instead that you have a sleep disorder, or a sexual dysfunction, or an eating disorder. And you may. But while those other things exist, they may be the symptoms of the depression, rather than the cause of it.

Some depressions start in childhood, and while they can be a purely inside biochemical form of depression such as bi-polar (which used to be called manic depressive disorder), more often depressions that start in childhood are a response to living in highly stressful circumstances including abandonment, abuse and/or domestic violence. Often this type of depression is "low grade," it makes a kid seem "flat" (which is called "dysthymic,") and the child learns to function around it, since often no one notices or can help. This type of depression can persist through the teenage years into adulthood. And in the way that brain and body so often work, what began as a sad response to living in an external situation of hopelessness can gradually become a phenomenon in your brain — it affects your brain's ability to produce enough brain chemicals to help you feel good. So you move through your life, but feel stuck with a certain level of low energy or hopelessness or lack of motivation or poor sleep. And of course, some folks are then more vulnerable to using food or alcohol or sex to give themselves a boost, creating more problems. By this point, resolving the outside triggers won't necessarily heal the inside depression. Sometimes appropriate medication helps; other times, psychological healing is what's most needed. Quite often, medication and psychological intervention together produce the best long-term healing.

These endogenous or "inside–triggered" forms of depression that we're talking about can also show up for the first time in adulthood. Sometimes we don't know why a biological depression arises in adulthood, but sometimes some very clear changes in biological markers accompany the expression of depression. Take Rosie, for example:

Premenstrual Madness: Rosie's Story

Rosie was a 37 year old administrative assistant and a single mom, with a passion for education, fitness and the outdoors, a flair for creative arts, and a strong spiritual life. She was reporting mood instability — feeling pretty good and stable a lot of the time, but then suffering through periods where she felt paranoid about her boyfriend's fidelity, irritable with her girlfriends, and just an overall hopelessness and desperation about whether she would ever have the security of a loving relationship with a husband. She had used all the tools she had to make a good life — had pursued education and career, had developed strong social supports, had fun recreational outlets, and had pursued a strong spiritual life through attendance at a church she liked, and through a real prayer life.

However, she had times when her desperation for a secure belonging led her to feel that none of her supports were enough. She found herself engaging in behaviors that weren't even congruent with her values: she had begun to cruise the dating and relationship websites (in spite of her awareness that she would have had a problem had her boyfriend done so) and when she and her boyfriend were on the outs she would engage in somewhat risky sexual behaviors while in the pursuit of the perfect relationship. As her goal of secure belonging eluded her, and as her other resources felt only sometimes helpful, she had begun to have periods in which she felt so overwhelmed that she contemplated suicide.

As quickly as possible, I helped Rosie begin to examine the roots of the problem. We saw that a poor attachment experience with her mom had left her vulnerable to feelings of rejection and abandonment, and prone to a yearning and pining for the *one* relationship that would make her feel better. I explained EMDR to her, and we decided that we would use this to heal some of the effects of her childhood that were making it difficult for her to self-regulate. We also planned to use EMDR to heal some of the later negative relationship experiences that Rosie ended up in (because her yearning for attachment had impaired her "radar" and made it difficult for her to choose good partners at times.) I also explained that we would need to help her heal her self-talk, the cyclical loop of inner narrative that reinforced her belief that she would never be loved the way she needed. And it was likely that these processes would help her use her already-rich spiritual life in deeper ways to stay balanced.

However, it was not until we had clarified what was going on in the First Domain- the Brain and Body — that we would be able to feel confident that healing in the other domains would be enough. We knew that had to be sorted out at the front end of therapy, so that our therapy process would be as efficient as possible. As it turned out, Rosie's biology acted even faster than *we* could. For one night (a week before her period, as it turned out) Rosie felt the rising tide of desperation and sadness, and knew that she was heading into the territory where controlling her moods could be an overwhelming challenge. As she thought about her loneliness and desire to be loved and cherished, and as her self-talk then took her in the direction of reviewing her failed relationships, she felt herself looking into a void that didn't feel like it could be filled. Up came the suicidal thoughts and feelings, and it wasn't long before Rosie found herself in the emergency ward of the local hospital.

Luckily, the medical staff put two and two together. They saw a 37 year old woman who *a week before her period* suddenly slipped from functioning to non-functioning, who went from enjoying her work, children, friends and spiritual life, to overwhelmed, lonely, hopeless, and suicidal. Her hormones were tested and she was found to have a dramatic lack of progesterone for this point in her menstrual cycle.

Those results warranted a once-per-week hormone test for the next five weeks (to track her through a full cycle), and sure enough, at the point in her cycle where her progesterone should be kicking in it wasn't. After ovulation, progesterone is supposed to increase for about two weeks, reaching about ten times its lowest level just before menstruation. Measurable increases should be detectable around day 21; that is, 21 days from the start date of a period. Since progesterone is a soothing hormone that helps with moods and sleep the lack of it would be a real problem for any woman, but would be *hugely* detrimental for a woman who had an underlying chronic source of sadness and some early life experiences that left her vulnerable to difficulties with self-soothing. In fact, both estrogen and progesterone create more receptors for serotonin and dopamine (two feel-good chemicals) throughout the limbic system, and they are therefore key in helping serotonin and dopamine to do their jobs (sleep and happiness.) So you can see that a lack of either of the two key female hormones could leave a woman feeling very unhappy. And remember, the limbic system is important in self-regulating, so a woman whose limbic system is lacking the help of her female sex hormones isn't just going to be unhappy—she's going to have a hard time regulating that unhappiness and her behavior.

You've undoubtedly heard of PMS (who hasn't heard a joke about PMS?) Well, this more severe form of PMS is called PMDD—that's short for Pre-Menstrual Dysphoric Disorder—and it's no joke. I've observed that both PMS and PMDD seem to be aggravated by poor nutrition and a shortage of essential fatty acids, and in my clinical practice I've seen them show up more in women whose brains and bodies were left vulnerable by early life trauma and abandonment.

Rosie was treated with progesterone, and her moods stabilized beautifully. She was prescribed progesterone to use the last week of her cycle, and she was able to feel normal. We were then able to do the healing in the other two domains where problems had been spotted — her history and her self-talk. Rosie was then able to manage herself, stay balanced, and integrate her healed self-concept and inner voice with her spiritual life. Her behaviors became congruent with her values, her impulsive sexual explorations ceased, she used and valued her social supports, and she became more optimistic about her future. Rosie was able to radiate a much more positive energy, and she felt unstuck, thanks to finding out that healing her biology was the missing piece that allowed her to get on with healing her underlying issues.

Hormones are just one of the sneaky factors that can underlie depression. Heavy metal toxicity from mercury, contaminants from well water and chronic candida infections can all trigger or worsen depression. (Candida albicans is the kind of yeast that can produce a vaginal yeast infection. If you have an unhealthy diet and a lot of stress, candida can move into other areas of your body and create a lot of health problems.)

Depression can also be hidden in women and girls who are afraid or unable to express sad feelings. This can be especially true for girls and women who didn't learn a lot of ways to self-soothe as they were growing up. They instead develop behaviors that look like rebellion, engaging in self-harming behaviors such as excessive drug and alcohol use or promiscuity. I've worked with poor young female victims of abuse who also just lived with their chronic unspoken depression, ending up as street kids, using drugs and alcohol to dull their pain, panhandling or prostituting to survive. A disturbing number of them had scars on their inner arms from multiple attempts at "cutting." Females are more likely than males to express their pain inwardly or toward themselves in these kinds of physical ways. Some also used tattoos or body piercings to express their sadness. (Not all tattoos or body piercings are an expression of pain, of course — except for the pain involved in getting them, that is!)

There are also quieter ways that women's depression can fly under the radar. Some women have lived with depression so long without processing it that they mostly experience it as lethargy, no energy, and they think it is associated with the high levels of domestic and family responsibility they tend to carry, so they stay stuck in it and disconnected from what it really is. And as they move into mid-life, they often think it is *just* their hormones (which may in fact be playing a role in the depression), and they may believe they just have to live with the lack of energy and optimism because it's a "natural" part of peri-menopause or menopause. As a result of this, when I see a mid-life woman in my practice who is complaining about low energy, fatigue, foggy thinking, and lack of pleasure, we always examine both her hormones *and* the possibility of depression. A surprising number of them have been put on anti-depressants without having their hormones checked. The medications don't seem to be working, and that's why they show up in my office. They may need hormones *or* an anti-depressant or *both*. (When a woman or man needs hormones, my preference is pharmaceutical-grade human-identical hormones. You'll often hear natural hormone replacement referred to as BHRT — Bio-Identical Hormone Replacement Therapy. Just know that bio-identical doesn't necessarily mean the same as human-identical. Ask your compounding pharmacy which they are using.)

How does depression hide in males? Males usually handle depression very differently from females. A lot of males don't have the internal "structures" or "schema" to identify for themselves their sad feelings (this is both a function of the way men's brains are wired, and the way we socialize men,) so they tend to *act out* their sadness. I have observed in my clinical practice that males are much more likely to convert their unexpressed sadness into anger or dangerous behaviors. I have treated lots of men who were convicted of crimes such as assault, aggravated assault, attempted murder, or murder. They have histories that are just full of sadness, and usually from early in their lives they had no way to process that sadness — they lived in abusive homes so saw and heard violence frequently, were often abused themselves, were shamed or ridiculed for showing feelings other than anger, and so they quickly learned to suppress their own sadness (huge amounts of sadness!) Then they began to act it out through bullying at school, picking fights, vandalism, theft and fire-setting. This doesn't excuse their choices, but it does point to depression and sadness as one important focus for our treatment of these men. These men, like almost all the men I see in my practice, need assistance to identify and express feelings in more effective ways. Until they deal with the covert (hidden) depression that lurks in their lives, they are at risk to have it keep them stuck, and to cycle through anger behaviors that can keep them in a life of crime.

Whether you are male or female, if you suspect that you may have some unprocessed depression, you will want to find out which Domains of healing will be most important for you.

Make the easiest Brain and Body change first: fix your nutrition. That way, if you need to see your doctor, medication will be able to operate in a more stable brain, and other tests for hormones or heavy metals or candida won't be complicated by symptoms of poor nutrition. And if you see a therapist, you'll be able to heal your history and learn how to manage your self-talk, knowing you won't undermine all your smart choices by bad nutrition. You'll also be better able to direct your energy and make use of some of the powerful (and pretty cool) metaphysical resources that are waiting for you to tap into.

Anger

You can see how talking about depression is a natural segue into talking about anger, especially after we've looked at how a lot of men convert sadness into anger. Unprocessed sadness or anger can be a powerful factor in keeping a person stuck, male or female. And just as it's true about depression, in a lot of cases there are some Brain and

Body factors that keep *anger* anchored, and keep a person (male or female) trapped and self-defeating.

Rage!

There is a powerful form of anger that can really get you in trouble, interfere with your ability to solve problems, communicate or even think straight! It is called "limbic rage."

Remember I told you that your limbic system regulates your emotional life, and that your limbic system is wired starting right after birth, through the quality of relationship you have with your caregivers. Some folks who had a really disadvantaged beginning in life have huge problems self-regulating. When anger comes up in their brain, primitive mechanisms take over, fight-or-flight chemicals start pumping, and they see red. They haven't yet developed the ability to intervene in their own anger response, so they don't look at solutions, they just explode. Some folks are aware of these levels of anger and don't explode but they feel overwhelmed and unable to participate in a meaningful problem-solving process.

It will be no surprise to you that poor nutrition can make this process much worse. Remember I told you that folks with ADD or ADHD need to be sure they have adequate, regular intake of protein in order to produce dopamine in their front brain to regulate in-coming information? And remember I told you that a healthy diet also produces serotonin, which calms the brain. Well, protein is also needed for the pre-frontal cortex to engage in some of its other functions, such as empathy and compassion, and the ability to foresee consequences and engage in long-range planning. So if you have a limbic system that already has a hard time self- regulating, and if you rob the brain of some of its most important fuel for empathy, compassion and foreseeing consequences, you can see how some folks would trip into limbic rage, not see or care who it would hurt, and go ballistic! Unstable blood sugar and/or

> unstable hormones can be other factors that make it very difficult to manage limbic rage.

So if you have an anger problem that is sabotaging you, and if your life feels stuck because you can't move past anger or its consequences, consider the above information as a clue to what may be the missing pieces of your life strategy. Healing limbic rage requires the help of a competent therapist or counselor, and it will involve strategies in at least three Domains: supporting your brain function, healing your experience, and arming you with smart self-talk strategies to keep you out of old patterns. My experience is that this is the best order to proceed through the Healing Domains: clean up the brain as quickly as possible, so that it can make use of deeper emotional healing, and so that it can then make sense of self-talk strategies. For folks who also are concerned about being able to use spiritual processes, connect with God or their Higher Power, and feel that the Universe supports them, they will then be able to do so, because the brain won't be sabotaging them, and emotional wounds and self-talk won't disrupt their ability to tune in to and receive good things at a higher level.

Bill's story is a great illustration of much of the above:

Rage: Bill's Story

Bill was in a heap of trouble when he was referred to me. He was a big scary-looking guy, aged 40, with a long criminal history of violence. He had been involved in the drug world, and was now forced to make a go of it in the straight world, and not having a lot of success. His involvement in the criminal justice system had resulted in him living in a supervised setting, with a lot of conditions on his behavior. Bill's biggest problem was a scary temper that had people fleeing from his presence (literally.)

And Bill knew that if he couldn't get his temper under control, his time in the straight world (and the free world) would be short-lived. Bill was having explosive bouts of anger that erupted up to ten times a day. His anger was the limbic kind we talked about in the box above. He would feel triggered, see red, and feel such blind fury that he would pound on the door of a bus if it arrived late, throw a grocery cart at the supermarket if it didn't work right, and scream curses so loudly and profusely that he had lost jobs and could now only work alone in a garage.

Bill's history was a tough one: he'd been adopted, then was pretty much ignored by his adoptive parents, and he had no real place of belonging. He felt sad, but had no healthy way to let the hurt out (in fact, didn't even know how.) In time, he acted out at school, got into trouble at school and in the community, and starting using drugs. Being high on marijuana was the only time he felt really good. (This is a really common pattern in men who show up in counseling with anger management problems.) His sadness and growing loneliness was never expressed, and in time he developed his explosive anger problem. (His lack of positive early attachment had left his limbic system vulnerable, and it was hard for him to self-regulate.) He also used food to self-comfort (easy to do when you're stoned and have the "munchies.")

But once Bill was under the watchful eye of the justice system, he no longer could use drugs. When he came to my office, he was at a loss as to how to control his anger. After I took his history *and asked him about his nutrition,* I knew that we would have to do healing in at least three of the four Domains. Bill's anger was clearly a learned behavioral response, but it was much more than that: his unprocessed sadness from early life experiences left him with a vulnerable limbic system, a lack of skills and confidence about belonging, very negative self-talk, and a tendency to eat all the wrong foods to comfort himself.

As I've emphasized in this book, if there are nutritional problems, we usually have to address them quickly, or much of what we do will be undermined or sabotaged. When I asked Bill what he was eating, he gave me a list of his favorite fast foods, all greasy and sugar-laden, and his favorite pop, of which he drank two liters (that's about two quarts) per day. And it showed: Bill was overweight, had unhealthy skin and hair, and he had a couple of other medical symptoms including terrible cramping in his legs at night (called Restless Legs Syndrome) and a neuropathy in his thumb (a deadening and pain in the nerve in his thumb, for which surgery was scheduled.) It was clear that Bill was so lacking in healthy nutrients that neither his body nor his brain were working right.

So we put Bill on a nutritional plan. He was skeptical, but willing to cooperate. He got help to grocery shop as he had no experience in choosing healthy food, and soon his cupboards and refrigerator were filled with fruits and vegetables, whole grains, and healthy proteins. When he went for fast food, he agreed to choose a salad with his burger, instead of fries, and when he went to a doughnut shop, he'd have a muffin instead of a deep-fried doughnut. He even agreed to replace some of the pop with water or sparkling water.

In two weeks, Bill's anger outbursts went from 10 per day down to one!

So we included a multi-vitamin, calcium and magnesium, and pretty soon the night-time leg cramping stopped. Then we added a B vitamin complex and he was even able to cancel his surgery because the neuropathy in his thumb disappeared. Bill was then able to go back to school, and he chose a food-related occupation!

We were then able to concentrate on healing his history, and over time, he also learned to listen to his self-talk and intervene in it. He was able to achieve more stable employment than in his past, to deal better with the frustrations of roommates and/or landlords, and to keep friends.

I've monitored Bill for years now (he sends me beautiful Christmas cards, and we have a session or chat periodically), and what we've seen is that as long as he eats properly he can maintain mood stability. When he strays from his optimal nutrition, he gets fatigued, cranky and irritable, and has paid the price a few times. So now, at mid-life, Bill "gets it" that to overcome his brain's tendency toward quick anger, to avoid blood sugar problems that can result in mood swings and diabetes, and to keep his job, he needs to consume healthy protein every four hours, keep processed sugars to a minimum, and drink lots of water. He knows that this makes it easier to intervene in negative self-talk, and to feel optimistic about his life.

Bill never returned to his life of crime, and because he found the missing pieces of his strategy, he got unstuck and got a life!

Addiction

Why is there so much addiction around us these days? It's another brain-and-body condition which can stand alone, or be layered on top of (or underneath) ADD, PTSD, anxiety, depression or anger. It can be easy to spot or it can be hidden. We used to think mostly of drugs and alcohol when we thought of substance addictions, but nowadays we also see widespread addictive behaviors with foods, particularly sugary, carbohydrate-laden foods and drinks, in kids and adults. And there are process addictions, too, including gambling and sex, and yes, texting on your hand-held wireless device. Compulsive, addicted behaviors are showing up in younger and younger people these days, including heavy use of video, computer games and television. Where is all this behavior coming from? And what do we need to know about the brain and body to help you fight addiction?

If you or a loved one has an addiction, there's really helpful information emerging that can help you plan a healing strategy. We have news about how the Brain and Body anchor addiction, and we also have important knowledge about how your History and your Self-Talk can keep addiction going. Good treatment of addiction should pay attention to all three of these areas.

The first thing to know is that some brains are pretty vulnerable to addiction. It's not known yet how much of this is hereditary, but we do see higher incidence of addiction if it exists elsewhere in the family tree. And there are a few areas of the brain that are easily primed to make you crave certain substances or processes. These areas form a "reward circuit" in the brain, and when they are activated repeatedly, the brain actually changes to keep those cravings going. Remember that earlier we spoke of the brain being "plastic" throughout life, and how that is a good thing because it means that the brain can repair itself in various ways. But it's also a bad thing if repeated use of an addictive substance or process induces long-term or permanent changes to the brain. Researchers are working hard to discover how to undo these dangerous circuits. Here's how the reward circuit works:

HOW YOUR BRAIN GETS ADDICTED

Everything that people can get addicted to, including alcohol, drugs, nicotine, caffeine, gambling, shopping, video games, sex, and even carbohydrates raises the level of dopamine in a part of the brain called the nucleus accumbens. The nucleus accumbens used to be called the pleasure centre of the brain, but it is now referred to as the reward centre of the brain. It's very closely tied to the amygdala and the hippocampus, which you may remember is the "limbic system," part of the emotional brain. Dopamine is the main neurotransmitter that activates this area. Sex boosts dopamine levels 50 to 100 percent in the reward centre! And the more dopamine the reward centre gets, the more it wants. Also, since the earliest evolution of our brain, cues that stimulate this part of the brain have caused it to pay attention to the possibility that our survival is in some way threatened.

So high levels of dopamine coursing through this area cause us to link whatever we are focusing on with our survival. So not only does the addict feel rewarded and pleasured by whatever is causing their dopamine boost, but comes to feel that in order to survive they *have* to have whatever that substance is or do whatever that behavior entails.

Other areas of the brain feed into the reward centre, and other chemicals play a role, forming a circuit. As this reward circuit is repeatedly exposed to the addictive substance, *or even to drug cues or to stress*, it restructures itself. It is now geared to the drug of choice more than to any other form of reward.

Signaling molecules called neuropeptides help parts of the brain to communicate. Current research with animals has found a neuropeptide called CRF (corticotrophin releasing factor) that mediates the addiction cycle. When CRF is blocked from release, relapse (or drug use) is prevented! In cutting-edge research, a variety of pharmaceuticals and even natural nutritional supplements are being used to prevent relapses in some forms of addiction!

It will be some time before these cutting-edge brain solutions are approved and available for general use, so in the meantime we need to help brains be healthy in other ways. One of the most important ways is to prevent and treat emotional wounds that set the Brain and Body up for addictions.

Where do these emotional wounds come from? Well, one of the most helpful sources of information ever to emerge about the roots of addiction has been the ACE Study, a huge study (17,000 Americans!) that took place from 1995 to 1997 at the Kaiser Permanente Medical Centre in San Diego, California. They found that *adverse childhood experiences* correlated with the incidence of different types of addictions. This means that negative childhood experiences showed up to a very high degree in the lives of people with addictions. This should not surprise you, given what I've already told you in this chapter about how the quality of early relationships we have with our caregivers sets up our brains to either self-soothe well or poorly. If you had negative or adverse experiences in early childhood, you can have a harder time regulating your feelings, and can be more vulnerable to addictive substances and processes because they give you a dopamine boost and *make you feel better*. The researchers at Kaiser Permanente looked at eight particular types of adverse experiences:

- Recurrent and severe physical abuse

- Recurrent and severe emotional abuse

- Contact sexual abuse

- Growing up in a household with:

  - An alcoholic or drug-user

  - A member being imprisoned

  - A mentally ill, chronically depressed, or institution-alized member

  - The mother being treated violently

  - Both biological parents absent

They found that the more of the above experiences people had, the greater their likelihood was of developing an addiction to smoking, alcoholism or injected drug use. (And it won't surprise you to hear that they also found that the more adverse childhood experiences people had, the more likely they were to develop a whole range of medical problems, social problems and depression.)

Dr. Vincent Felitti, who authored the study, has said that the study suggests that the basic causes of addiction "lie within *us* and the way we treat each other."[1]

So, if you are vulnerable to addiction, you need to be sure your life strategy focuses on the First, Second and Third Domains. That means:

---

1 Felitti, Vincent J. (2004). *The Origins of Addiction: Evidence from the Adverse Childhood Experiences Study.* Department of Preventive Medicine, Kaiser Permanente Medical Care Program, San Diego, California

- You need to be sure you are taking care of brain and body. A malnourished brain is more vulnerable, so good nutrition is needed to support good brain chemistry. And since stress is a known factor in triggering drug use for some people, you need to reduce stressors and have effective stress-reducing strategies.

- You need to heal whatever wounds or "leftovers" you are dragging around from adverse childhood experiences, to reduce your vulnerability to stress and depression. That way, you won't have to rely on big hits of dopamine from addictive substances to make you feel better.

- You need to be sure that self-talk is working *for* you, not against you. Learn how to manage your self-talk by reading Chapter Three and/or by talking to a good cognitive-behavioral therapist. Also, check out a Twelve Step group such as AA, NA, SA, or CA where other recovering addicts will tell you about the lies they've told themselves, and how they've learned to change their thinking. Check out the links in the Appendix for addiction recovery supports.

- You will then be able to explore and benefit from the Fourth Domain, if you want to check out or improve how a higher power can assist in recovery. Either way, you'll radiate a more healed energy capable of attracting to yourself more of the kind of life you desire.

Sexual Addiction

People make jokes about sex ("how bad could it be to be addicted to sex?...") but it really is no laughing matter. When people come to see me with uncontrolled sexual impulses, they usually are in despair and at their wits' end. They come from all walks of life, and generally are pretty nice people, often with good education, jobs and careers. But their lives have become unmanageable because they are constantly planning for their next fix of some form of sex, and are preoccupied, distracted, feeling guilt and shame, and have often sacrificed huge (even stunning) amounts of money and time to feed their addiction. Many have lost their relationships and marriages because of their deception and covert behavior, and/or because after they've been caught, they promised not to do it again, and they were caught again.

Sexual addiction often starts with internet pornography and chronic masturbation, and can include inter-active on-line sex, or it can be completely off-line and include affairs, prostitutes, and massage parlors. Some individuals struggle with behaviors in all those areas. Sexual addiction can start in childhood, not just adulthood, and it is present in males and females.

At the heart of sexual addiction is an intimacy problem. What I most often see in folks with sexual behavior problems is that they are using sex to self-soothe, to fill the gap where real intimacy should be. Why? Well, often because they grew up in families that weren't able to teach intimacy skills, especially emotional intimacy and closeness. Parents do their best with what they themselves were taught, and often they are preoccupied with adult problems and also just don't know how to create a tone of emotional intimacy. As we talked about earlier, if the emotional intimacy or attunement wasn't there between infant and parent, the child's emotional brain wires in a way that can leave it vulnerable to self-regulatory problems. As these kids grow up and are exposed to the dopamine "hit" that happens with exposure to sexual stimuli, they can easily become dependent upon sex to fill the emotional void they feel. The availability of internet pornography has fed into the problem (since it provides the dopamine "hit," along with pseudo-intimacy in some cases.)

So sexual addiction becomes a problem that is rooted in all four Domains: it is a neurochemical phenomenon, it may have some of the genetic roots that are hypothesized to underlie many forms of addiction, it can show up in folks whose emotional brains were not well-wired for intimacy or self-soothing in childhood (and it is thus often an outcome of adverse childhood experience), it is fed by self-talk (and accompanying behavioral choices) and it is often accompanied by a spiritual void. This is why when I see a sex addict, we focus on all four Domains. We work hard to stabilize any Brain and Body conditions that may be at play, we do EMDR to heal History, we use cognitive-behavioral techniques to intervene in self-talk, and we link the addict to peer supports that help him or her to persevere in practicing new self-talk and new behaviors. The best peer supports are often found through Twelve Step programs such as SA (Sexaholics Anonymous), SAA (Sex Addicts Anonymous) or SLAA (Sex and Love Addicts Anonymous.) Sexual addiction therapy is a specialty and should only be undertaken with a professional who has proper training. Look for a therapist who has a CSAT designation (that's short for Certified Sexual Addiction Therapist.) Some therapists who have an ATSA designation may also be able to help you. (ATSA is short for Association for the Treatment of Sexual Abusers. ATSA therapists are specialists in helping people who have compulsive sexual behavior problems, including those with criminal sexual behavior problems.) See the links in the Appendix for more information.

Because sexual addiction is still not well understood by people, there can be a lot of confusion about what sexual addiction *is* and what it is *not.* Jennifer's story is a great example of this:

Sex Addict? Or just Hormones?: Jennifer's Story

Jennifer was a beautiful, smart 38 year old investment dealer, with solid values, good friends and a strong spiritual life. She had an on-and-off boyfriend with whom she was having a few problems, and she occasionally had some business stressors. She came to see me because she was worried about her sexual behavior. She reported that although other things in her life were going pretty well, she seemed to be constantly preoccupied with sex. She wanted very frequent intercourse, and needed several orgasms daily (through intercourse or masturbation) in order to feel relieved. This didn't exactly fit with her values for a balanced life, and it was disturbing her that she couldn't seem to manage her own sexual impulses better. I took Jennifer's history, and saw some clearly unresolved painful experiences from the family she'd grown up in. I also saw that she had developed some stringent behavioral standards for her life (her way of exercising some control, given that she'd grown up in an environment in which she had little control.) I wondered how much of these were operating in her difficulties with her boyfriend, and how much these factors could be setting her up to both need self-soothing and at the same time create self-shaming about her choice of self-soothing behavior. I also knew that I would need to examine all four Domains, in order to plan effective treatment, and as you've seen in this book, I most often start with the Brain and Body, since biology can play the most surprising role in behavioral and emotional problems. So I advised Jennifer that we would be wise to test her hormones as a starting point, and that we could start other treatment while awaiting the results (since there were definitely issues in the second Domain.) We ordered saliva hormone testing (see the box below for why we chose saliva testing) and when the results came back, we were both pretty surprised. Jennifer had testosterone levels *significantly* above the top of the normal range for a woman in her age group, and these were creating a high biological sex drive.

I knew that in order to be sure that this high biological sex drive wasn't also being fed by a need to self-soothe we would have to do some basic healing in the second Domain, so we proceeded with EMDR to resolve her painful childhood and family experiences. She experienced significant healing about those issues, and then felt ready for us to address the problems with her boyfriend. We used the Imago Dialogue, which is a form of relationship therapy that is widely respected around the world. (I'll tell you more about it in Chapter Two, and give you links to learn more in the Appendix.)

When Jennifer and Tom had developed a reliable set of skills to maintain a healthy cooperative relationship, Jennifer came back to see me on her own. She reported that her sex drive was just as high as ever, but that now that she felt more peaceful about her family and childhood, and now that her relationship wasn't a source of stress, she felt her sex drive was in a balance with other areas of her life, and she didn't always need to act on it. Jennifer had a strong belief in God, and she felt that God had made the most of her high testosterone levels by using them to propel her into therapy where she would heal deeper issues in her life. This fit with my "gut" instinct, my clinical impression of Jennifer. She was capable of genuine intimacy, didn't have other areas of compulsivity in her life, and overall just didn't meet the criteria for sexual addiction (we use a test called the SAST, the Sexual Addiction Screening Test to help us determine this. An on-line version is available, and the link is in the Appendix.)

Hormone Testing

I want to be clear that I don't do hormone testing for everyone who thinks they might be a sex addict, or for everyone whose behavior suggests they might be. I *do* use hormone testing when pieces of the puzzle aren't naturally fitting together, and/or when someone is at mid-life and complaining of some of the other kinds of symptoms that we've talked about earlier in this chapter, like depression and insomnia (or ones we haven't talked about, like weight gain.)

I also use hormone testing when a young person who shouldn't have depleted sex hormones is complaining of overwhelming fatigue and lethargy, or report they've been diagnosed with chronic fatigue syndrome or fibromyalgia. Sometimes it turns out that they are in adrenal burnout, and have depleted levels of cortisol and DHEA, two major adrenal hormones. And the really great news is that most of these hormones can now be replaced with human-identical hormone replacement therapy (although lifestyle changes are always needed too when someone is in adrenal burnout.) Hormone testing can be a really critical piece of figuring out how to get someone unstuck.

So let's take a look at the saliva method of hormone testing, since it was so helpful for Jennifer:

SALIVA TESTING

You've probably had a few blood tests done over the years. They can be incredibly helpful in ruling out concerns, and in diagnosing medical conditions. In addition to blood tests (which are often referred to as "serum tests"), tests can be conducted in urine, stool and hair. Perhaps the most helpful test that I have used in my practice is saliva testing for hormones.

You see, hormones tend to ride around on the backs of binding proteins in your blood stream. Not all of these hormones necessarily make it into your cells where they can be biologically active. So when you have a blood test done, you may not be getting an accurate reading of how much hormone is actually operating in your tissues. You could look like you have high or normal hormone levels, but not really be getting the benefit of them. (One reason is that our bodies produce HBGs, hormone binding globulins, which accompany hormones through the blood stream. If there are high levels of HBG, our hormones may not be as active as we need.) On the other hand, when you spit into a test tube, the hormones in your saliva have had to make their way from your blood stream into your tissues, including saliva gland tissue, and then into your saliva. In other words, a saliva sample gives us a very good picture of how much hormone is actually operating at a tissue level.

Saliva testing laboratories can test almost the complete range of women's and men's hormones, as well as a couple of the hormones which indicate whether your adrenal glands are in good shape — those hormones are DHEA and cortisol. When we use these tests in treatment planning, we can often save valuable time, energy and money by properly targeting biological issues which can be major sources of stuckness. And when we have the Brain and Body operating with appropriate levels and types of fuel, we are more efficient at solving other problems, and able to be more confident that healing will "take" and that you won't get stuck in the same way.

For more information about saliva testing, check out a few links that I have provided for you in the Appendix.

Medication Mess-Ups

Is your prescription the right one for you? If not, it can contribute to Brain and Body imbalances, and leave you frustrated, ill and stuck. Incorrectly-prescribed pharmaceutical and herbal remedies are a widespread but often hidden problem. They can waste your health-care dollars, mask your symptoms and create new symptoms. Why does this happen? Because all too often, in these days of overloaded health care systems, inadequate time is taken to properly assess a patient, *get a complete list of the patient's medications,* consider drug interactions, and consider other intervening factors such as diet. Although they do their best, many physicians lack adequate nutritional training, and many alternative health care practitioners lack adequate medical training. The patient becomes the testing-ground, or is given a "default" commonly-prescribed medication or remedy because there is pressure to treat people quickly and move them through (and out of) the system. A patient can be prescribed a medication or remedy that is completely inappropriate to their circumstances, no one notices, and complex new symptoms develop. The patient is then prescribed further medications to fix the "new" problem, but their condition worsens, and gradually their life spirals out of control. No one realizes why this person is so ill.

William found himself in that situation:

Medication Mess-Up: William's Story

William is a warm, imaginative, and thoughtful man, retired from practicing law. At age 66 he experienced the loss of his spouse in tragic circumstances, and it undid him. But William did everything right when it came to his grief work. He reached out to friends, to mental health professionals, engaged in bereavement groups and individual therapy, read widely on the subject of grief, and worked hard in the first year of his bereavement to gradually address the challenges of dealing with his wife's possessions, her remains, and eventually, her estate.

William challenged himself to adjust to his new life — he exercised, investigated spiritual pursuits, improved his computer skills, and tried to think a bit about the future.

William was at late mid-life, and he was under stress. He had a history of high blood pressure, so he was on a calcium channel blocker, and a couple of other blood pressure medications. He had asthma, so he was on a nasal spray and another medication. And even though his acute grief subsided, not surprisingly William found himself depressed, and so he was prescribed an anti-depressant. And William had a heck of a time sleeping, so his doctor prescribed him sleeping medication. And somewhere in there, about a year into his bereavement, William started to develop terrible anxiety. He'd feel it when he got up in the morning, and it would grip him at various points during the day. He tried to change his self-talk, to no avail. He tried to use his spiritual tools, with no relief.

He'd had EMDR to deal with some of his grief, and that had been helpful, but it didn't put a dent in his anxiety for some reason (which is odd, because EMDR is extremely good at treating anxiety.)

William talked to his doctor, and sure enough, he was put on anti-anxiety medication. William was now on nine prescription drugs! And his anxiety got worse.

What to do? Well, a long and careful review of the side effects of all of his medications revealed that the well-known sleeping medication he'd been prescribed, when used in aging patients, produces anxiety! William had been suffering what is known as "iatrogenic illness," which means illness caused by medical treatment! William was both chagrined and relieved at the same time, and he began a supervised program of gradually titrating down off the sleeping medication, (which was causing the problem), and the anxiety medication (which hadn't helped anyway.) (He found a compounding pharmacy that compounded his medications into ever-smaller doses, so that his body acclimatized itself to the gradual withdrawal of his highly addictive sleeping medication, as well as to the withdrawal of the anxiety medication.)

It took several months, but William lost his anxiety symptoms. And with some changes to his diet (such as no caffeine), and a carefully selected nutritional supplement, William began to sleep better.

With the missing piece of the puzzle in place, William was able to get unstuck. His Brain and Body could now support him in all his other efforts to heal. He was able to work through more of his grief, practice his new spiritual learnings, and move forward in his new life.

There are models of medical practice that would have saved William a lot of grief, and there is one emerging model of medicine in particular that can help you take care of yourself in the more positive and preventative ways that William and many others have come to prefer:

SMART MEDICINE

Functional Medicine is personalized medicine that deals with primary prevention and underlying causes instead of symptoms for serious chronic disease. It is science-based, focuses on your biochemical individuality, is patient-centered, looks at health as a positive vitality (not just the absence of disease), and it addresses the inter-connectedness of your organs so that they work together (rather than addressing your heart, or your kidneys, or your bowels all separately, for example.) Functional Medicine pays attention to your hormones and neurotransmitters (such as brain chemicals), your immune system and the role of inflammation in illness and disease.

It also focuses on nutritional and digestive health, including your ability to absorb nutrients from your food, and on whether you have a healthy balance of flora in your body (flora are good micro-organisms that line your digestive tract.) It addresses imbalances in your body, whether at the level of your cells, or in larger systems like your musculoskeletal system.

Functional Medicine[2] uses the patient's *story* as a key tool in the diagnostic process. This means you will be listened to! Check out the Appendix for links so you can learn more.

---

2 *IFM: The Institute for Functional Medicine*, 2009. Website: "About IFM: What is Functional Medicine?"

Looking After Your Brain and Body

By this point, you may have a few ideas about some of the most common ways your Brain and Body could be sabotaging you, or at the very least slowing you down. I haven't remotely exhausted the list of the ways that hidden conditions can undermine your efforts to live well or to generate positive energy and attract back positive outcomes. However, what I hope this chapter does do for you is awaken you to the powerful role that your brain and body can play in keeping you stuck, and that it can play in your healing.

Before we take a look at smart ways for you to take care of yourself so that you can attract the life you desire, let's check in with Julie Jones, so I can tell you what we did for her Brain and Body, and how it helped her to start getting unstuck:

More on Julie's Story

Remember Julie from the beginning of this chapter? Julie was a stressed-out, depressed, lonely woman with financial and housing and employment problems, was afraid of burning her friends out, wasn't responding to medication, and didn't seem to have spiritual tools up to the challenge of her life. I knew we'd have to get Julie ready for deeper healing by addressing her issues in the Brain and Body first. As it turned out, she had a lot of those issues: she wasn't sleeping well, had digestive problems, allergies and constipation, cold sores and slow wound healing, forgetfulness, low blood sugar, and weather-related migraine headaches! Since I suspected Julie had malabsorption problems (because allergies and chronic stress can interfere with nutrient absorption), we looked carefully at having Julie take some nutritional supplements to support her body. She started a multivitamin and an herb called Rhodiola right away, and then 5HTP shortly thereafter. (Both are calming nutritional supplements which also elevate mood and can promote better sleep.)

For occasional anxiety, she also began to occasionally use L-Theanine, which is an extract from green tea. (You should not take these or any nutritional supplements without supervision from your health care provider.) Julie also eliminated caffeine. One week later she reported that her mood states were much better, and three weeks later she reported that she felt more grounded, less anxious, much less depressed.

Julie's settling biochemistry allowed us to get ready to focus on deeper healing. We'll come back to Julie later, and I'll tell you about which parts of her history we knew we needed to heal and how we did it.

⁓

To support you in your efforts to have as much health as possible in your Brain and Body, and therefore to ramp up to higher levels of living, let's summarize some of the most important things you need to be doing for your biological self, especially if you are in a slump or really stuck. It's vital for your Brain and Body to be receiving the support they need along with any other solutions you may be trying, or you could waste valuable time, energy and money and still feel unable to move forward.

As soon as we've summarized these Brain and Body essentials, we'll delve into the Second Domain of Healing. And with these essentials under your belt, you'll be able to make good use of whatever healing processes you decide to explore in the Second Domain. Here's to good health!

My Top Seven Brain and Body Strategies

1) Nutrition, Nutrition, Nutrition!

No surprise that this is number One. Eat three to four times a day, always starting with breakfast so that you have alertness, concentration, blood sugar control and weight control as soon as you start your day (breakfast really does fire up your metabolic furnace and set you up for brain control and weight control.) Be sure to include:

- Healthy protein such as fish, poultry, lean meats, dairy and/ or tofu, omega 3 eggs, and beans for blood sugar control and alert brain function. (Include nuts if you're not allergic to them. And raw nuts are better for you than roasted ones, if you have access to them. Raw nuts have to be kept refrigerated, though, to prevent their oil content from spoiling.)

- Complex carbohydrates in the form of well-washed fresh fruits and vegetables, and whole grain breads, cereals, pastas or brown rice (or potatoes with skins on) for energy, vitamins and for the fiber that controls blood sugar and bowel regularity.

- Healthy fats, including olive oil, flax seed or oil, and fish oils, all of which perform protective functions for the heart and brain, and which help your body produce hormones.

- Filtered water throughout the day, and enjoy a cup or two of green tea (or rooibos, a South African herbal tea) for their anti-oxidant properties. Reduce or eliminate caffeinated and/or sugared beverages.

- Wherever possible, consider eating organic foods to reduce your intake of pesticides and chemical fertilizers

- Wherever possible, choose whole food instead of food that has been broken down into another form (so choose fruit instead of juice, whole grains rather than polished grains, vegetables instead of vegetable juice.) You'll get more nutrients and more fiber.

- Reduce or eliminate processed foods including sugar, white flours, trans fats, deep-fried foods and artificial colors and flavors. These are the foods that produce "free radicals" which stress your cells, weaken your immune system, and speed up your aging.

Messed-up Molecules, Crazy Crystals

Foods that have been highly processed, super-heated, deep-fried, hydrogenated and/or which have artificial additives usually are characterized by the fact that their molecular structure has been distorted. That means that when you eat those foods, you are asking your cells to take in unnaturally-shaped molecular chains — just like trying to fit a bent key into a lock. What results are toxic by-products called "free radicals" that harm cells and stress the body, and set the body up for disease states. And if you think about it, since you are a molecular being emanating an energy field, what do you suppose toxic foods do to your internal energy system and your external energy field?

In a fascinating photography project done by Japanese scientist Masaru Emoto[3] in the 1990s, it was discovered that molecules of water are affected even by our thoughts, words and feelings. Emoto's photographs show frozen water crystals after they had been exposed to positive or negative energies, and the results are nothing short of astonishing. Water exposed to negative energy froze into twisted, distorted and gruesomely-shaped crystals. Water subjected to positive energy froze in stunningly beautiful forms. Since you are composed of 70 percent water, it would make sense to expose yourself to the most positive energies and external influences you can, in order to maintain cellular health and an "alive" energy field.

Food and water are not only fuel for your Brain and Body, but they are a powerful medium from which your energies emanate. Nourish yourself in the direction of your dreams!

2) Fitness!

Research is revealing an incredibly strong link between exercise and the ability to reduce troubling symptoms of ADD, ADHD, PMS

3 Emoto, Masaru (2001). *The Hidden Messages in Water*. New York: Atria Books.

and PMDD, to name just a few. It's really clear that exercise actually primes the neural pathways in the brain, increasing levels of important neurotransmitters, and increasing communication between those neurotransmitters. This means that exercise is a cheap (free!) way to treat and even prevent some medical conditions. And of course, you already know about exercise's positive effects on your heart health, sleep, weight, and ability to help the brain stay young.

So, find any kind of enjoyable physical activity that you can fit into your life, at least five times per week for 20 — 30 minutes. It's best if it makes your heart beat fast. It can be walking on a treadmill in front of a comedy show on TV, running up and down your stairs as you listen to your favorite music, playing in the yard with your kids, jumping on a trampoline, playing paintball with your kids, tennis, aerobics, Pilates, yoga, housework to fast music, the wii Fit, and even sex! Work as much of your fitness into your day as you can — take the stairs instead of the elevator, say no when they offer to carry your groceries to the car, walk to the store for milk, get on your treadmill when you're gabbing on the phone. Most people find it best to avoid exercise late in the day as it can disrupt sleep (though moderate exercise *during* the day can promote sleep.)

Your body will thank you for any efforts you make, because you'll not only open up the blood flow that keeps your heart, brain, and body healthier and younger, but you'll release endorphins which make your brain feel happy! ("Endorphin" is short for "endogenous/inside morphine," and that's why exercise can produce a natural high.)

3) Protect and Stimulate Your Brain

- Protect your brain by wearing a helmet when skiing, biking, rollerblading, playing baseball, rockclimbing, or in any other situation where projectiles are flying or you could fall. Wear your seatbelt in your vehicle. I've lost count of how many people I have treated for anger management problems (and other "self-regulation" problems) who had a head injury in their history!

- Stimulate and protect your brain by varying what you expose it to. Where possible, avoid long stretches at the computer, or in front of the TV or video games. In order to be sure that you use and exercise different parts of your brain, and to give your children's brains every advantage in learning and attention, match every half-hour that you or they spend in front of electronic screens with activities that are physical, interactional (i.e. involve other people) or that use other senses. (Physical and interactional play also help to ensure that children develop their social skills, whether it's cooperatively building a fort with a friend, or playing board games with a sibling.)

- Avoid recreational drugs. Your brain is not resilient to crystal meth or Ecstasy, no matter what you think. Crystal meth carves holes in your brain, and Ecstasy depletes one of your most important brain chemicals — serotonin — which can leave you edgy and subject to rage. Cocaine and heroin, even though they are naturally-derived, can devastate your body and brain. Overuse of pot or alcohol can impair your energy, concentration and motivation, and interfere with any healing or life repair strategy that you undertake.

4) Nutritional Supplements

- Sadly, much of our agricultural land is so over-worked that it is depleted of nutrients, and food grown on this land lacks the vitamin and mineral content that it had a generation ago. Talk with your health care provider about using a good multi-vitamin to supplement your diet, and prepare to be surprised at how much more energy you have, how much better you sleep and how much healthier you feel.

- Consider fish oil capsules as an additional source for DHA, one of your brain's most important nutrients.

- There are some smart natural supplements that can target specific brain and body problems. Certain amino acids like L- Tyrosine can improve concentration in mild to moderate ADD, and supplements like 5HTP can support mood function and sleep in people whose serotonin systems are underperforming. Check out the links in the Appendix to some well-respected websites, where you can get more information.

- If you aren't eating well enough (no matter what your mother tells you!), consider anti-oxidant supplements such as Vitamin A, C, E, selenium, grape seed, quercetin, resveratrol, lycopenes, and lutein. Talk with a health care provider who has a good knowledge base in nutrition to see if any of these should be added to your diet.

- And if you're still not eating well enough, consider having a "green" drink daily. There are a variety of these nutritional drink powders available now, and they are a great way to protect your brain and body.

5) Balanced Hormones

- As you've seen in this chapter, hormone imbalances don't just happen in mid-life. You must have healthy fats in your diet to produce hormones, and a good diet can go a long way toward preventing hormone imbalances at all stages of life.

- If you appear to have a mood disorder, or are at mid-life and not feeling great, make sure that your health care provider or therapist give strong consideration to the role that hormone imbalance could be playing. Consider asking for hormone testing. Check out the links in the Appendix for saliva testing laboratories, and consider saliva testing as an alternative or adjunct to blood tests.

- Check out whether BHRT (Bio-identical Hormone Replacement Therapy) or human-identical hormone replacement therapy are right for you if you have blood or saliva results that show a hormone deficiency. (Obtain hormones from a reputable compounding pharmacy, and only if you have medical tests that show you need supplementation.) More and more people do not want the side effects of synthetic hormones in their bodies, and we are fortunate to have these newer alternatives to consider. Talk with a variety of health care practitioners and check out the links in the Appendix to get more information.

6) Medication — Well-targeted, carefully dosed, and only when necessary!

- Be an educated consumer. If medication is recommended to you, speak to your pharmacist. They can provide you with information about side effects, and interactions with other drugs and foods.

- Follow dosing instructions exactly.

- Advise your health care provider if you experience adverse effects. Ask if there are alternative medications or strategies to consider. For example, some people with Seasonal Affective Disorder (SAD) find that their depression lifts if they use a Full Spectrum Light or an LED desk lamp every morning, and they can use lower doses of medication, or in some cases, may not require medication. Also, some people find that their herpes can be completely controlled with the natural amino acid L-Lysine (combined with a diet that has a higher proportion of foods containing L-Lysine and a lower proportion of foods containing L-Arginine) and they can avoid medication completely.

- If you are taking medication for a mood disorder, you may be one of the people who can use it for six months or so, then titrate off it, and never need it again. (Titrating off should only be done in consultation with your health care provider, and should always be gradual to allow your body to adjust. You can get into trouble by going off your meds too fast!) However, you may be one of the people who, after going off meds, finds that even with great nutrition, great counseling or therapy, positive self-talk and strong spiritual tools, you just slip back into your mood disorder within a few months. Don't beat yourself up!

More and more people these days seem to be lacking the adequate supplies of brain chemicals that produce healthy moods. Some people find that cycling on and off meds a couple of times a year (with medical supervision) works well for them. Some people find that they require a consistent dose of their medication to stay stable. If you have done everything else to promote health, you may find that medication is *your* missing piece of the puzzle.

7) *Meditation, Prayer, and Mindfulness*

Strategies that produce a positive energy within you and a positive energy field around you will support you in achieving the life you really want to attract!

- Research shows that meditation increases theta brainwaves (theta waves are slow and relaxed, and also happen as you transition from waking to sleep.) So meditation is great for sleep and lowering your blood pressure, and it is a wonderful tool for directing your mind toward manifesting the kind of life you want. (In Chapter Four we will look at very cool ways that you can use your mind to influence external events, and to support you in creating your desired life.)

- Research shows that prayer can facilitate healing, and it can even influence the output of agricultural crops. Prayer can calm you, strengthen you, and can help you manifest surprising abundance. In the next few chapters, we'll focus on what you might need to heal if you're not having results with this spiritual tool, and we'll also look at some out-of-the-box forms of prayer that really make things happen!

- Mindfulness is a very simple practice, involving just slowing yourself down and being really present to what you're doing or seeing or hearing or smelling or touching. You just breathe in a relaxed way as you stay present to whatever you're doing. It's a way of meditating while you walk, sit, stand, work, clean the house or drink a cup of tea, or engage in any normal daily activity. And if your mind wanders, you just bring it back to the feel of your feet on the floor, or the swish of the dishcloth inside the pot, or the smell of the orange, or the sun slanting through the window, or...

Chapter Two

WHY CAN'T I JUST GET OVER IT?

The Second Domain of Healing: Your History

> *"What lies behind us and what lies before us are*
> *tiny matters compared to what lies within us."*
> — attributed to Ralph Waldo Emerson,
> poet, philosopher, orator, innovative thinker

RALPH WALDO EMERSON was right when he said your history is a tiny matter. Your History *doesn't* matter much, but only if you have taken steps to ensure that the negative influences of your past are neutralized and transformed. Otherwise, your History is so *not* history. Without good healing, your History is not past, not over. It is with you now, and *so* potentially influential over your future. Your past experience can cling to you, create your internal energy system, and radiate an energy field around you. Your past experience sends a ripple effect out through time, into your present, into your future. And we want only the positive influences from your History (or the positively-transformed ones) to have that far-flung an effect.

When we heal your past, we neutralize *what has already happened.* When we heal your past, we change its rippling effects out into time and space! And amazing discoveries in quantum physics suggest something even more mind-bending:

QUANTUM SURPRISES ABOUT YOUR HISTORY

Don't forget that you are a molecular entity, or energy slowed down, and so everything you do or experience is an energy transaction. Everything you think, every action you take occurs because energy makes it possible. And no energy in the universe ever disappears; it can only transform into something else. All things that have ever happened, are happening or will happen occur through energy, and all of them exist in some way in what is called the Field, the infinite sea of vibrating energy of which time-space is composed. These events are all enfolded in what the British physicist David Bohm called the "implicate state," [4] and not necessarily in a linear order, but rather as a sea of probabilities. Since the time of Einstein, scientific research has clarified that the position of the observer changes "reality," and later research has even suggested that it is the *choice or intention* of the so-called observer that effects which probability manifests, and therefore which "reality" comes into being.

So here's where it gets mind-bending: quantum scientists have conducted research in which individuals were asked to use that choice or intention to influence events about which they had no knowledge, but which had *already happened*, and the data gathered demonstrated that research subjects were in fact able to influence which probabilities played out! American scientist William Braud has speculated that there are "seed moments," which are the initial moments of a chain of events, and that human intention can be directed back in time to those seed moments, to act upon the how a set of conditions will *later* play out! [5]

---

4 .Bohm, D. 1980. *Wholeness and the Implicate Order.* London: Routledge.
5 Braud, W. 2000. "Wellness Implications of Retroactive Influence," *Alternative Therapies in Health and Medicine,* 6(1): pp.37-48

From this perspective, what we can do in therapy or in any true healing process is to neutralize what was! We can bring new meaning to what was, influence how the probabilities of your life play out, and change the meaning and effects of the original experience!

And even if we set aside the quantum perspective on your experience, we know that healing past painful experiences changes lives, and changes what's possible for you.

So, let's say you are taking good care of yourself, you've addressed any potential biological problems, and your Brain and Body are in harmony, but you're still stuck. That's a clue that you need to look at the next Domain of Healing: Do you have some History that's still playing out, still unhealed? Because if you do, it can be limiting your well-being, undermining the otherwise powerful effects of a balanced Brain and Body, rippling out into your quantum field, messing up your internal and external energy fields, and influencing how the probabilities of your life will play out.

So, in this chapter, we're going to answer three important questions:

- How do you know if your History is keeping you stuck and interfering with attracting a great life?
- How do you heal your history?
- How can you be sure it's healed?

1) How Do I Know if my History is keeping me Stuck?

In this section you'll see how we figured out how to help Julie Jones get unstuck by looking at the four main questions below. These are the things you'll want to keep in mind as you look at your own life, as they'll help you get clearer about whether an overlooked factor is holding you back:

- What are the necessary ingredients of a good childhood?
- What childhood and teen experiences create baggage?
- What adult experiences, including traumas, create baggage?
- What do baggage or "leftovers" look like?

We'll start with the factors that create a positive childhood. In the box below you can read about the ingredients which create quality of life during childhood, and which lay the foundation for a healthy adult life:

THE INGREDIENTS OF A GOOD CHILDHOOD

A secure attachment with a parent or caregiver. Another way of saying this is that we need good bonding with a parent or caregiver. This sets up the optimal brain wiring we talked about earlier, and leaves us more capable of trust, intimacy, optimism, and the ability to self-soothe or self-regulate in appropriate ways. It sets us up for an energy of positive expectancy; we radiate out our belief that we are loved and lovable, and so we send a message into the molecular field that attracts more of those kinds of relationships.

Safety. That means having our physical needs met, being protected from dangerous people and situations, having our boundaries respected, being taught to set our own boundaries, protection (as much as humanly possible) from traumas like physical and sexual abuse, and assistance to address problems. These safety experiences "prime" us to use our radar wisely, to be adept at screening out boundary-violators. They also leave us with a stored sense of security that creates a relaxed energy within, and which radiates out an openness to life. Our channel is able to be open to the healthy possibilities around us in our world, and as we learn to access the quantum universe.

Good role modeling. That means seeing cooperation, healthy trust, problem-solving skills, and seeing people manage their anger. It also means seeing how a person can be both independent (autonomous) and interdependent at the same time, so that we'll know how to stand on our own two feet and still have closeness, but not get enmeshed or co-dependent with someone. This sets us up to conserve energy—to not waste energy having to make a series of relationship mistakes. And so our energy is automatically available for bigger things: to radiate out and attract back the kind of "high order" experiences that dreams are made of.

If you didn't get some or most of these things in childhood, it has likely contributed to the way probabilities have played out in your life, and chances are that it's still messing up your energy and contributing to you feeling stuck in one or more ways in your life.

Childhood Detours

Detours slow you down. Every life has some detours, and we can learn some great things from a detour. But when you're a kid, emotional detours just slow you down and get in the way of growing up. To do well in life, we need to move along a "developmental curve," or a "developmental path." When we do, we grow through several important stages, and each stage of development builds on the completion of the last one. If things got in the way of you developing trust, intimacy, optimism, a sense of safety, a sense of your own personal boundaries, or the development of your problem-solving and anger management skills in your childhood, it's like a tree has fallen across your developmental pathway, and it's going to slow you down. You'll spend a lot of energy or time trying to climb over the obstacles in your development, and you can get a bit bruised or scratched as you do so. If the obstacles that fall across your path are really big ones (I'll give you examples shortly) you can end up deviating off your developmental path completely, trying to find a way around the block, and it can really slow you down, make you lost, and even prevent you from resuming your progress down the developmental path (so that you often feel or act like a kid, or are accused of doing so.) And as you might suspect, this would limit future probabilities and possibilities.

Big and small intrusions in your developmental path can end up being some of your biggest teachers, once they are healed. But in the short run they suck energy, weaken your foundation and cause you to stumble around, trying to compensate for what got lost or interrupted. Because *make no mistake*, developmental intrusions must get healed or they will be dragged forward *ad infinitum* (forever!) Healing them is the only way to transform them into wisdom, and turn them from a liability to an asset.

WHAT ARE THE DEVELOPMENTAL STAGES?

Many famous psychologists and theorists have identified the stages that we move through in our development. You might have heard of some of them. Erik Erikson focused on our social and emotional development, Freud of course focused on our psychosexual development, Kohlberg charted our moral development, and Piaget mapped the stages of our cognitive (thinking and knowing) development. Regardless of how many stages they identified, they all agreed that we do best in one stage of development if we have completed the work of the stage that came before it, and that that happens when we have the best love and support and modeling in each stage.

> Another innovative thinker named Abraham Maslow[6] went on to say that in fact we can only self-actualize (reach our potential, live fully) if we have previously received four major building blocks, one after the other: the meeting of our biological needs, then safety, then love, then esteem. Each one builds on the one before it, and allows us to have the resources and completeness to focus on living a great life:
>
> Able to Live Big!
> Esteem Needs Met
> Love Needs Met
> Safety Needs Met
> Food and Shelter Needs Met
>
> MY VERSION OF MASLOW'S HIERARCHY

Childhood and Teen Experiences that Create Baggage

So what experiences get in the way? What events interfere with laying down the foundation of our life, disrupt our developmental pathway, cling to us energetically, and then contribute in a major way to being stuck? Well, basically anything that interferes with bonding or attachment, safety or good role modeling, especially in childhood, but later as well. These experiences can include:

- Abandonment or rejection, including losing a parent through death when we are young (or having them go to jail or hospital for a long time)

- Witnessing domestic violence, chronic conflict or a cold war between your parents

- Being physically or sexually or verbally abused or witnessing it happen to your siblings

- Being scapegoated in the family (being the one who is blamed or shamed for everything)

6 Maslow, A.H. 1971. *The Farther Reaches of Human Nature.* New York: Viking.

- Living with parents who have addictions, mental illness or severe depression.

Sound familiar? It should. It happens to be pretty similar to the list of experiences that the ACE Study (from Chapter One) found to be the most important contributors to addictions. It doesn't mean that if you have the above experiences that you'll have addiction. It just means that we know these experiences impact a child's development in a lasting way unless they are healed.

We know that they are traumas, even though some of them might have been stretched out over a long period and you got used to living with them.

Are there other experiences that can hold us back? Yes, there are some other traumatic experiences that happen either alongside the above experiences, or by themselves in the midst of an otherwise pretty good childhood. If we're getting what we need at home, we're more likely to cope with them and adapt to them. If things aren't so good at home, they're more likely to end up as long-term baggage that slows us down:

- Being bullied at school, or being seriously picked on by a teacher

- Witnessing a crime, or witnessing or being caught in the midst of a hold-up, a mugging, a murder or suicide, a fire, flood, tornado, hurricane, earthquake, a car accident, etc.

- Moving a lot, and not getting a chance to make or keep friends

- Being hospitalized at a young age, especially if it was repeatedly or for lengthy periods or if our parents or caregivers didn't or weren't allowed to visit

- Losing a beloved grandparent, relative or pet, especially if we didn't have other sources of love.

Once we have one or more of these wounds, we aren't as resilient to other stressful experiences, our energy gets taken up by dragging our baggage along, it starts to affect the way we look at the world, and we aren't as ready to move into the next stage of development. There's a domino effect, and everything else gets tougher. And you can squash this stuff out of your consciousness, but you can't erase it out of your brain or body, so there's a part of you that remains *stuck at the age you were when the trauma happened!* A part of you never gets as fully grown up as you deserve to be, your energy field carries the wounds of the child, and your best efforts to live well don't get you where you want to go.

Adult Experiences that Create Baggage

You were shocked. You weren't ready. You didn't have support. You weren't believed. Your livelihood, health or safety was dramatically affected. If this describes any of your major life experiences, there's a higher chance that they become baggage or cause stuckness for you. Never assume that because you've "put them out of your mind" that you can put them out of your body. And a happy childhood doesn't necessarily make you immune to the effects of adult trauma either. Although it's true that fortunate people who have pretty happy childhoods tend to be more resilient to traumas and bad experiences — and seem to attract fewer of them — even they can carry long-term effects from trauma. If you feel stuck, you need to check out whether the types of experiences listed above are playing a role.

Some folks have teenage and adult traumas that are layered on top of unresolved childhood experiences, and they are more likely to be slowed down or even completely undone by these later events. But among these folks, many do not necessarily have a clear perception of a string of bad things happening in their life, since they may be so accustomed to things not working well over many years. Just as we talked about in Chapter One, where biological conditions can fly under the radar, so too can unresolved life experiences. To these folks, it's just one more job loss, or bad relationship, or unwanted sexual experience, or betrayal or disappointment. Because of this, I learned years ago in my practice not to just look for the obvious teenage and adult traumas such as sexual assault, being "dumped" in a major relationship, or being a victim of crime or medical trauma. And I learned to not just work on what people reported as their worst traumas, because often people have become so numb to their own experience (or it's become normalized to them because there is so much of the same around them in their neighborhood or culture) that they can't really identify why they feel so depressed or hurt or angry or just plain stuck.

So when I train other therapists, I advise them to focus on healing a person's history *right from the beginning,* right from childhood, (wherever possible) because this is the best way to get at the roots that underlie and anchor a lot of adult trauma. And amazingly, especially when we use EMDR, healing the earliest negative experiences often produces a healing "spillover" onto adult life, and there's often much less adult material to take care of. If there are still specific adult experiences that need healing (such as sexual assault, an accident, being a victim of crime, a cheating spouse) they heal much more easily and thoroughly.

So to repeat, whether you have had a pretty good life and have been pretty resilient, or whether you feel like life has been one long string of trials and tribulations, if you are feeling stuck you need to check out whether you have any of these types of experiences still unresolved:

- Shocking or untimely events
- Experiences where you had no support
- Experiences where you weren't believed
- Experiences that dramatically affected your livelihood, health or safety

The next section will give you clues as to whether any of the kinds of childhood **or** adult experiences we've talked about are getting in the way of a great life.

What do Baggage or "Left Overs" Look Like?

What goes around comes around. Bad experiences from childhood or adulthood can keep showing up in the following ways, *unless we get them healed*:

- They can get "stuck" in our cells and our central nervous system and start to "repeat!"

- They can contribute to a negative inner "script" or tape that loops endlessly in our brain, contributing to very bad feelings, and shaping our behavioral choices

- They can form a negative inner "template" or model that shapes our behavior and propels us towards more of the same!

- They can mess up our boundaries, allowing in unhealthy people and experiences, or making us so closed and rigid that we can't allow in the healthy input we need

- They can mess up our energy, so that we radiate an unhealed energy, and can't attract what we dream of.

Here's how that happens:

Baggage in the Form of Trauma Stuck in the Body

A Vietnam veteran was walking down the street. A traffic helicopter flew overhead. The vet freaked out! His auditory nerve had been triggered, it fed into a stored sensory memory in which the sound of a helicopter meant war, and so he was no longer on a city sidewalk, but rather standing in the killing fields of Vietnam. This is a flashback. This is what happens when trauma gets stored in the body. When Vietnam vets returned home from war, many had terrible flashbacks of combat experiences and reacted to day-to-day events as though they were still in danger. Researchers and clinicians who worked with them learned that even minor (and even unconscious) reminders of traumatic experiences can re-awaken that trauma in the brain and body. Thanks in large part to Vietnam veterans, it's now understood that when that happens, the body activates alarm mechanisms, spews stress chemicals, chews up hormones, causes the brain to screen out other incoming information, sets up an unconscious reaction to an external event with alarm or fear, and finally triggers anger, avoidance or desperate measures to avert the perceived danger.

This means, for example, that if you were abandoned when you were young and helpless (even if you don't remember it!) that trauma can cause you to react with fear and panic any time your brain thinks you're going to be abandoned again (e.g. if someone close to you is gone too long or appears disinterested in you.)

Rosie, whose story of severe PMS you read in Chapter One, is a great example of this. Because she had abandonment experiences in her childhood that left her fearful, anxious and lonely, her wiring was "primed" to expect other experiences just like that, so any time a boyfriend or friend didn't pay enough attention to her, it re-awakened the stored experience and she reacted with the same primal fear and desperation she felt as a helpless child.

Have a look at the following diagram to see how that happens:

Here's What's Going On Inside Your Brain

When an Unresolved Trauma gets Activated:

! Information comes in that in some way seems like earlier
trauma **even if there's no actual danger**

It goes to 2 places in your Brain:

First:	*Second:*
Your Amygdala	*Your Pre-Frontal Cortex*
(Your Alarm System)	*(Your Rational Brain)*

It turns the information into an
Emotional Signal

↓

Your Amygdala, believing
there's danger, activates areas
in your brainstem where your
behaviors, your nervous system
and your hormones kick in

↓

You feel as though your Trauma
is happening all over again,
so you feel abandoned, or
threatened, or attacked, etc.
and you REACT

It evaluates whether there's
danger, then informs the
amygdala, but the amygdala
has already reacted
emotionally

(The Good News: EDMR therapy heals this kind of reaction.)

Baggage in the Form of Negative Self-Talk

Your brain wants to make sense of things! So, after a trauma (or even just day-to-day negative experience), our brains try to figure out what happened. Because we have a "thinking brain" — the cortex of our brain makes us think and the left hemisphere of our brain is programmed to make meaning out of things all the time — we start developing an inner "story" to make sense of an experience. And we start to add all kinds of things to that story, like "it's all my fault," or "I'll never be loved," or "people will always abandon me," or "I'm not good enough." And we unconsciously or consciously re-play that tape or CD in our heads, and pretty soon it's part of our world view and belief system. It shapes the choices and behaviors we engage in. So now, on top of some wired-in body reflexes that can re-play physical and emotional aspects of our traumas, we also have a cognitive, or thought process that anchors our story of danger or lack and keeps it repeating. That "voice" or story begins to predict and shape our future.

Baggage that Creates Messed-up Relationship Radar

If your father, for example, kept abandoning you, then you now have an inner "template" or model that unconsciously sets you up to expect that experience with adult males. And not only that, but human beings engage in a process called "recapitulation" in which we unconsciously seek to re-play a negative experience so that we can master it. So a person who has experienced abandonment may unconsciously set up dynamics in their relationships where they "test" whether they'll be abandoned again.

So we have the original trauma, the negative self-talk that gets layered on top of it (in a well-meant effort to try to make sense of things), and now a distorted template inside that skews our radar for healthy relationships. We end up on automatic pilot, zeroing in on what is familiar, or we desperately try to avoid what got modeled for us. But if we don't have the healthy alternative template inside, many years of painful searching and experimenting may ensue as we try to produce a relationship different from what we were exposed to in our family.

Baggage that Shows Up as Messed-Up Boundaries

Emotional, physical and sexual boundaries are learned first in the family. They govern interpersonal behavior. If healthy boundaries are not modeled in the families we grow up in, we may not learn an appropriate sense of our privacy, of our right to physical space, of the right to accept or reject certain kinds of touch, or of the need to respect other people's boundaries, space, confidentiality and privacy. If we have lacked healthy modeling of boundaries, and/or if we have been subject to boundary violations (verbal, physical or sexual), it can be hard to know where to place our own boundaries with people, or how to set them when we *do* know where they should be. Boundaries can then be either sloppy (weak, diffuse, too permeable, enmeshed) so that we aren't asserting, protecting or even defining ourselves, and/or we are invading others' boundaries. Or, our boundaries can end up too rigid (closed, isolating, controlling) so that we can't receive the information, support, caring and experience that will help us to be healthy people, and we can't offer those things to others.

Often, people whose boundaries have been violated during their formative years find that it becomes hard to gauge when, where and how to set boundaries. So a person who was abused in their family, for example, can find themselves with boundary problems, because trust, intimacy, sexuality and family roles get all mixed up. Without effective boundaries, they can easily be re-victimized or can violate the boundaries of others. And on top of this, the trauma can get re-activated at a cellular level if they are reminded of it, their self-talk can be full of mistrust, fear, and/or anger, and their inner relationship template can keep attracting similar types of predator-victim relationships.

Messed up boundaries are really common; they are one of the biggest issues I see in my practice every day, in folks from every walk of life. I have a favorite book that I recommend to people — it is the book that has helped more people in my practice than any other, for many years. It's Anne Katherine's *Boundaries: Where You End and I Begin.*[7] Get it for yourself or a friend.

Baggage that Messes up Your Energy Field

It's easy to imagine what all of the above does to a person's energy. The energy field is now radiating need and fear, (or poverty and lack, or shame and guilt, or anger and aggression) and so it can't attract the healthy love that is longed for. And with a bleak energy circling around us, it's tough to reach through it and access higher energies and resources such as a higher power or a connection with the divine. And so we stay stuck. We become a magnet for all that we don't want.

These processes I just outlined for you can be repeated in hundreds of ways: if you were shamed as a kid (that's your trauma), then you start to believe you're defective (that's your self-talk), then you gravitate to people who end up replaying that dynamic with you (that's your inner relationship template acting like a magnet for more of the same), your boundaries are messed up, so you can't protect yourself from these similar experiences, and you radiate a low energy and have trouble using your tools to attract what you really want. Stuck!

Or: you witnessed chronic conflict between your parents (that's your trauma), then you start to believe that all relationships are like that, or that you have to yell to make yourself heard, or that intimacy isn't safe, (that's your self-talk), then you either avoid relationships like the plague or you go into them and repeat what you've learned (that's your inner relationship template messing up your ability to create something better, and your confused boundaries allowing in more of the same), and your energy field carries that disturbance and recycles it, so you

---

7 Katherine, A. 1991. *Boundaries: Where You End and I Begin.* New York: Simon and Schuster/Fireside.

never attract the healthy fun partnership you dream of. Stuck!

Here's one more: you witnessed one parent constantly put down the other parent or one of the kids in the family (maybe you.) That's your trauma. Without realizing it, you gradually come to understand that one person gets to be the "boss," the judge of what's true, and the other person can't be right, or confident or strong at the same time (so even if you don't hear those thoughts loudly in your head, they're there and they're operating.) That's now your self-talk. And your inner template for relationships acts like a magnet to attract similar dynamics, so you keep finding yourself in jobs where you're not respected or heard, or in apartments where your landlord doesn't keep his promises about what he'll fix, or friends who borrow your stuff and don't return it, or... So you repeatedly find yourself powerless, your boundaries aren't protecting you, people pick up on the vulnerable energy that you emanate, and your energy field draws in predatory or bossy "users."

And of course, it isn't just family wounds that set us up this way. Let's say you were sexually abused by a babysitter or a stranger when you were younger (that's your trauma). If you couldn't tell (because of threats, bribes, fear or shame), or if you did tell but weren't believed (a believing parent is the single biggest factor that influences a kid towards a healthy resolution), then your self-talk gets going in the direction of "people will hurt me, I'm not safe, my body is defective, I'm dirty, I'm powerless, it must be my fault, etc." Your radar for who's healthy can get a little messed-up, and so even if you've had a reasonably healthy template for relationships, it can get hard to sort out whom you can trust. Your boundaries can be a little confused — too loose at times, or too rigid at times. Your energy field is one of vulnerability that predators pick up on, or one that is self-protectively closed, and so you are limited in what you can attract back. And the wound keeps operating, keeping you stuck.

To fix your energy field, you'll need some healing to address the original wound. Then you'll be able to make great use of some new tools such as empowered self-talk and strong boundaries, and your radar will operate more effectively. Your inner template will start to point you in the direction of healthier people. Your energy inside and out will reflect your sense of well-being, as well as your increased confidence, self-esteem, and ability to trust wisely. That's how you'll get unstuck.

———————

Let's check in with Julie Jones again, so you can see how her baggage and leftovers were operating in her life:

Julie's History

When we last checked in on Julie, we had identified a whole host of body symptoms that were giving her trouble, and we had stabilized her Brain and Body with some carefully selected nutritional supplements. We were now ready to focus on how her History was playing itself out and creating trouble for her. You'll remember that Julie was depressed, lonely, in an unsupportive work environment, had financial difficulties, a bad landlord, and was worried about burning her friends out. She also had a history of bad boyfriends. Well, it turns out that Julie was raised in a family where her parents had had pretty inadequate parenting themselves, and they were overwhelmed with a number of children. Julie was one of the middle children, which meant that her needs kind of got lost in the shuffle. (Birth order can affect how children are treated in the family, and how they experience themselves.) Julie's parents were pretty unhappy people: her mom was passive and overwhelmed, and her dad was angry, depressed, and could be physically aggressive. Julie observed their relationship and didn't see a healthy model of a woman being assertive or experiencing intimacy. Because the kids had to compete to get their needs met, they were often in conflict, and resented one another. Julie became the one they blamed for things, and in time she became the official scapegoat for the whole family.

So it's pretty easy to see what the traumas were in Julie's life: an attachment wound that left her depressed, anxious, and with low self-esteem, some physical abuse, and being scapegoated. From those unhealed experiences she developed her self-talk, her inner script that told her "I'm not sure I'm smart or attractive, I won't be treated well, I'll probably have to settle for less, I don't know who I am, I'm not sure I want others to know me, etc." And that self-talk informed a lot of the behavioral choices she made, it became the message she was beaming out to the world, and it became the predictor of her experience.

And on top of it, her inner relationship template was to attract a guy who wouldn't treat her well, and to subjugate her needs to his. That template also acted like a magnet for work and social situations where she would be unsupported, and even for housing where her rights would be violated. Because her boundaries weren't strong, she'd feel angry but unable to fix it, so slide into depression.

And Julie became just like the cartoon character who walked around with the little cloud of dust over her head. She radiated a depressed, hopeless, vulnerable and angry energy, and so could only attract more of those conditions. She couldn't reach through the fog to larger energy or spiritual solutions, and she felt very stuck. Soon you'll see exactly how we addressed each one of these problems.

Now you have a general idea of how "leftovers" or baggage can play out in your central nervous system, your self-talk, your inner model or template for relationships, your boundaries, and in your energy field. And you have a sense of how Julie's experience caused certain kinds of leftovers to play out in her life. So let's look closer at how certain experiences can produce very specific types of leftovers. And don't be worried if you see yourself in this list — it's a signpost pointing towards healing. If anything below sounds familiar, you'll have a clue about whether your History is in the way of the life you desire:

Attachment Leftovers

- As you know, the earliest trauma is often the lack of attachment by a parent, affecting your limbic wiring (no surprise), and leaving you vulnerable to problems self-regulating: addictive or compulsive behaviors around alcohol and drugs (especially if addictions already run in your family), and with sex, gambling, or spending.

- The lack of attachment can leave you reactive —poor frustration tolerance, easily angered, limbic rage (so you intimidate or victimize others), or milder versions that look like a heightened sense of injustice, or being critical or judgmental. It can also result in fear of abandonment or being prone to anxiety (so you look for a caretaker or develop control behaviors.) Some people are prone to a whole combination of these, affecting their personality development, and ending up with what are called "borderline" symptoms or full-fledged Borderline Personality Disorder. They can feel particularly overwhelmed at times and be vulnerable to suicidal impulses. See the Appendix for two great books to help you understand BPD and to cope with a loved one who has it.

- A lack of attachment by a parent can leave a child lacking the "mirroring" or positive interactive experiences that help to form a healthy personality, and so the child mirrors him or herself by becoming very self-focused or "narcissistic." We call this a "narcissistic wound." If you are often accused of being very "all about yourself" you may have a narcissistic wound.

- The lack of attachment can leave you afraid to trust, not knowing how to be intimate, so your relationships are on-and-off/come here-go away or keep falling apart. You may repel people, or you may seek a caretaker and become overly dependent on them, or co-dependent and enmeshed with them.

- Lack of attachment by your parent, or outright emotional abuse can leave you with depression, low self-esteem, emptiness, and so you can become withdrawn or needy.

Trauma Leftovers

- Traumas like physical and sexual abuse can leave you with body image problems, hate for your body, lack of comfort with touch, uncertain of good physical boundaries so you have trouble protecting yourself, or a tendency to invade other people's boundaries. Sexual abuse can leave you with a host of vague, generalized pelvic complaints, including pelvic inflammatory disease (P.I.D.), urinary tract infections, sexual dysfunctions such as vaginal clenching and trouble lubricating (vaginisimus and dyspareunia), or erectile difficulties (premature ejaculation or impotence) or trouble with orgasm (inorgasmia.)

- Experiences of chronic or repeated trauma can cause you to develop a dissociative mechanism in your brain, that causes you to "zone out" or space out, or shut off, and it can happen throughout life whenever you're stressed, or if your brain is reminded of your trauma. For some people, this results in D.I.D. (Dissociative Identity Disorder) in which they split off parts of themselves to self-protect. (It used to be called M.P.D., or Multiple Personality Disorder.)

Physical Leftovers

- Attachment and trauma leftovers, and/or living in chronic stress in your family can create learning problems, activate auto-immune problems, and set you up to be more vulnerable to illness of every kind. You can end up with migraines, eczema, bowel problems and all kinds of what are known as inflammatory conditions because stress raises the acidity levels in your body and that creates the conditions for inflammation and disease. You can end up with teeth problems such as tooth-grinding (bruxism) or even tooth stress fractures if you chronically clench your teeth. You can end up with TMJ (Temporomandibular Joint problems) if you chronically clench or carry stress in your jaws. If you have a host of physical ailments that recur, or that doctors can't find a cause for, or if you have long-term insomnia or repeated stress-related illnesses, you may benefit from doing some healing on your growing-up experiences.

Leftovers that Look like Independence

- Some folks with strong survival skills (they often get described as the one who was the "resilient child" in their family) have managed to self-correct and transcend a lot of the conscious effects of childhood. If this is you, you may have learned to create a certain amount of safety, security and independence for yourself. But you may find you can't seem to go beyond, to fulfill your potential, self-motivate, find the kind of relationships you want, or dream a dream for your life. If this describes you, you may be someone who has unconsciously learned not to ask for too much, and learned to do everything on your own. You may not even be aware of any of these types of problems in your life, but that could be the clue to what's not working: you may have learned to be so excessively self-reliant or self-sacrificing that your filters unconsciously screen out help and support. The missing piece of your life strategy may be *to adjust your boundaries to ask for and to accept the support you deserve.* Consider having a life coach or therapist help you move beyond where you are — you deserve it.

Leftovers that are just leftovers

• You've had an identifiable trauma not relating to your family experience, such as being a victim of crime or a natural disaster, or a cheating partner, or a medical or financial disaster, and you continue to be unable to sleep well, or your appetite or sex-drive have been affected, or you're overusing alcohol or you have become fearful or anxious. (This happened to a lot of people after the crash of the stock market in late 2008 and early 2009). You may have post-traumatic stress or full-fledged PTSD. EMDR is the best therapy for an efficient resolution of these symptoms.

The leftovers identified above give you some clues about whether you need to heal your History. It is not an exhaustive list, but it is a list of the most common ways that we can "wear" our History. If you are "wearing" any of these signs and symptoms, or if you are stuck in any of the ways we looked at in Chapter One, then you can be sure that they are messing with your energy, both inside and out. They are interfering with you being able to vibrate the healthy, alive energy that attracts good people and great things. They are likely messing up your connection to the larger Universe in which you find yourself, and blocking you from effectively using the powerful energy and metaphysical tools that create the kinds of outcomes you are yearning for. It would be smart to look into some good healing.

2) How Do I Heal My History?

There are some great ways to put the past into the past, for good. Your History can sometimes be healed through relationships, and often through good counseling or therapy. So how do you go about finding what you need? Well, I want to narrow down the search for you, so in a minute I'll give you my top tips for the smart consumer. But just before I do, for people who like to know how things got started...

WHERE DID THERAPY COME FROM?

Cave dwellers didn't have therapists. As far as we know, early societies just focused on surviving. They used the support and care of their families for a sense of well-being. Then along came religion and magic—as agricultural and industrial societies developed, life became more complex, and people who developed mental health issues began to seek help from practitioners of alchemy or religion. Rituals such as exorcism and prayer were used. Later, practitioners of medicine were enlisted to treat "madness."

By the late 18th century, along came an innovative thinker named Franz Mesmer, who began to look into whether there were more scientific explanations for well-being. He eventually declared that a magnetic force or "fluid" within the universe influenced the health of the human body, and he theorized about an "animal magnetism" that operated within people. His ideas were somewhat ahead of their time, and so the principles and methods of his so-called "Mesmerism" did not find widespread acceptance. (Although we still use the word "mesmerized" to describe when someone is entranced or enraptured with something.) Some of Mesmer's ideas about magnetic or force fields influencing health would later be echoed in energy-based healing practices such as Reiki and qi gong.

A few of Mesmer's ground-breaking concepts were utilized a few decades later by a Scot named James Braid, in a healing process Braid called Hypnosis. Clinical Hypnosis came to be an established method for treating psychological and medical problems, and it is today recognized by the American Psychological Association, and by the American Medical Association. (Clinical Hypnosis is different from the kind of hypnotism-for-entertainment you may have heard about. Although a certified hypnotherapist uses some of the same principles, they'll never ask you to squawk like a chicken!)

Parallel to developments in hypnosis, another new form of therapy emerged. Developed by Sigmund Freud in the late 19th century, it would lay the groundwork for the way some therapy is done today. It was simply called "the talking cure," and it came to be the major form of healing practiced by psychiatrists. People really did lie on couches and simply talk. Their analyst sat out of view and listened to their free association about various subjects. Over time the process came to be known as psychoanalysis or analysis.

However, later practitioners such as Alfred Adler and Carl Jung introduced more organization into the process of therapy, using concepts of psychological development and change. Their healing method, which focused on psychological processes, came to be called psychodynamic therapy. The Freudian constructs used in psychodynamics, such as the ego, the id and the super-ego, are still helpful and in use today in many kinds of "talk therapies." Carl Jung's methods of dream analysis are still in use too, and they are incredibly helpful (and interesting!)

By the 1920s, behaviorism came into favor as a "scientific" approach to healing. It remained the dominant form of therapy for at least thirty years, and it used behavioral conditioning and social learning to facilitate change. You may have heard of early experiments by behaviorists such as Ivan Pavlov, who used Classical Conditioning to train a dog to salivate when it heard a bell ring (believing that dinner was on the way.) (People refer to the automatic repeating of learned behaviors, or responding automatically to a cue as being like Pavlov's Dog, and now you know why.) You've also probably heard of B.F. Skinner, who was one of the major figures in the field of behaviorism, and you may have heard of animal research by behaviorists, which helped shed light on human behavior and how it is reinforced or conditioned by reward and punishment.

By the 1950s, people began to seek help to look within, and sought more relational methods of healing. Along came the humanistic movement, which was based on the Existential writings of Rollo May and Viktor Frankl (he's the famous survivor of the Holocaust) and on Carl Rogers' Person-centered psychotherapy. The relationship with the therapist now became very important as an agent of change.

Also the "here and now" became as important as the past, and new therapies such as Gestalt, developed by Fritz Perls, came into being in the 1950s. Gestalt essentially means "wholeness" in German, and to promote wholeness it borrowed concepts from psychoanalysis, Psychodrama, Eastern religion, and others. Many therapists use Gestalt techniques by themselves, or in conjunction with other kinds of therapy today.

Around this time, two very powerful new therapies were born: Rational Emotive Behavior Therapy, developed by Albert Ellis, and Cognitive Therapy, developed by Aaron Beck. These therapies were combined into Cognitive-Behavioral Therapy in the 1970s, and CBT as it is called is still widely used to help people change their beliefs and make new behavioral choices. In Chapter Three, we'll use a form of it to help you undo some of the disempowering thoughts that keep you stuck.

Since that time, the mental health field has incorporated systems theory (which was in use in the biological and mechanical worlds) and evolved a form of therapy for groups and families. Systems therapy is most often encountered in Family Therapy.

And parallel to these developments in the first half of the 20th century, some specific forms of group psychotherapy came into being. Jacob Moreno developed Psychodrama, in which people play out unresolved issues with the help of a group. And Irvin Yalom published his groundbreaking ideas about the principles and practice of Group Psychotherapy.

There are now therapy groups all over the world for all kinds of problems, and group therapy is often used as an adjunct or additional support to individual therapy.

Transpersonal psychology also came into being, focusing on the spiritual dimension of human functioning.

And individual therapies have come to include feminist therapy, somatic (body-centered) therapies, and expressive therapies such as art and dance therapies. There is a whole discipline called Play Therapy for children.

In the late 1980s, EMDR (Eye Movement Desensitization and Reprocessing) came into being. It has been described as a "power" therapy that triggers changes in the brain, and allows individuals to deeply release and heal negative experience. Cutting its teeth with Vietnam Veterans and sexual assault survivors, EMDR proved its capacity to resolve Post Traumatic Stress Disorder, is recognized by the American Psychological Association, and has come to be used around the world for an astonishing variety of psychological, emotional and physical traumas.

And since that time, we've also seen the development of Energy Psychology, which complements much of the wisdom of transpersonal psychology. Energy Psychology looks at the human energy field (the electromagnetics of the brain and body) and its relation to emotion, cognition, behavior and health. It uses concepts from Eastern and Western medicine, and it has given birth to a number of emerging energy therapy methods, most of which are still experimental. Some of these methods are referred to as "power therapies;" you may have heard of Thought Field Therapy (TFT), or Tapas Accupressure (TAT), which use deceptively simple processes to mobilize healing in the body, or procedures such as "muscle testing," which allow the body to communicate to the client and practitioner.

Healing Your History through Relationships

It's kind of fitting that since some of the biggest wounds happen in your earliest relationships, that some of the biggest repair can happen in later relationships. However, this is not something you have a lot of control over: you can't just order up a healing relationship and then say, "there, it's all good." What happens for some people, by luck or divine intervention, is that they get adopted or fostered by really loving parents early enough that some of the attachment wound effects are balanced out by nurturing, acceptance and belonging. Others suffer through their childhoods and teen years, and then happen to find a pretty healthy nurturing, loving partner who helps them "catch up." However, usually *you can only attract a partner who is as healthy as you are,* so if you're walking around with wounds, you're likely to attract a partner who has their own share of unresolved stuff. And besides, it's not your partner's job to be your therapist.

Some people luck into surrogate families — a group of friends, a friend's family, or later, in-laws who reflect back to them their worthiness and beauty and who help them to "catch up." This can accomplish a lot, as long as you don't burn out these supports.

Some folks find their reparative relationships in Recovery settings such as Twelve Step groups and treatment programs. They find peers who unconditionally accept and care for them and they get a chance to work through some of their trust and intimacy issues in this setting. However, this can be a minefield — there are lots of folks in recovery who are in a pretty wounded place, and when your inner template meshes with theirs, a dysfunctional relationship forms that perpetuates the original wounds.

If you've got some pretty significant wounding from your childhood, it is usually difficult to have a complete healing with any of the above forms of reparative relationships. What these relationships can do is prepare you so that you can make use of professional help to address the deepest or most complex or most entrenched aspects of your wound. And these relationships can be a great form of support while you are in therapy.

If it is a specific trauma you need to heal from, such as a car accident or a natural disaster, relationships aren't usually an effective source of resolution. In those cases, an EMDR therapist is probably your best bet. And when you find a good counselor or therapist, you'll discover that it's not only the therapist's techniques that heal, but that a relationship with a caring therapist helps you heal too!

A Brief Consumer's Guide to Therapy

Where to Find Therapy

Is finding good therapy like looking for a needle in a haystack? It doesn't have to be. Most cities and many towns have public service agencies or non-profit agencies that offer basic counseling if you cannot afford private therapy. They often have a sliding fee scale, may offer you the assistance of seasoned clinicians or interning student therapists, and are often limited to offering very short term treatment. Depending upon your issues, you may also be referred by your doctor or hospital to a psychiatrist, psychologist or social worker who provides services within the health care system. In these cases, the psychiatrist may be limited to addressing diagnostic and medication issues with you, and/or the therapy services you receive may be shorter than you require. You may be referred for group therapy within the non-profit or medical systems, because they are efficient ways of delivering service. Take advantage if it is offered to you, but also be aware that you may require individual counseling or therapy to address the issues which cannot be adequately or privately dealt with in group.

If you prefer the option of therapists who are in private practice, it is often safe to rely upon word-of-mouth recommendations from people you trust and/or who've had helpful counseling. But you can also contact state or provincial associations or regulatory bodies for listings of accredited, licensed therapists. Check your yellow pages or the internet.

Therapists and Counselors

Therapists can be a joke. At least, they are in the movies. They're decked out in spectacles and surrounded by dusty books, or through a cloud of incense they're telling you to "get in touch with your feelings." In movies like "What About Bob?" the disinterested psychiatrist just keeps telling his patient to "take baby steps." The poor patient tries to figure out what this cliché means, and how to do this without clear and practical help. As funny as the movie is, none of us wants to be that patient. Fortunately, in real life there are lots of consumer protections to prevent this scenario from playing out. And there are lots of ways to be sure we're getting a first-class professional who will compassionately, wisely and skillfully help us to heal and grow.

So what do you really need to know if you're going to look for a counselor or therapist? First of all, you might wonder whether there's a difference between a "counselor" and "therapist." Well, there are numerous types of mental health practitioners, including psychologists, clinical social workers, psychiatrists (they are medical doctors), pastoral care workers (including ministers and pastors), nurse therapists and family therapists, to name some of the most common.

Some of these practitioners may refer to themselves as counselors, and some as therapists or psychotherapists. The ones I've listed here have usually completed a Master's or Doctoral degree and may have additional training, but *not all people who simply have degrees in the above fields are necessarily qualified to do counseling or therapy.* For example, there are psychiatrists who only assess, diagnose and prescribe medication, there are industrial psychologists who work in career counseling, and there are social workers who are community organizers. Licensed practitioners who identify themselves as counselors or therapists have typically completed specialized education and met professional requirements that allow them to be chartered or registered as clinicians by professional associations and regulatory bodies.

It's important to find out if your therapist or counselor is licensed, as it's your best assurance that they are required to operate according to a Code of Ethics, are required by law to have Continuing Education to stay current in their knowledge base, and may be covered or partially covered by various healthcare plans.

COUNSELOR OR THERAPIST?

It's not really important whether a licensed mental health professional calls him or herself "counselor" rather than "therapist." I tend to think of counseling as "giving counsel," or giving advice, and I tend to think of therapy as the process of "remediating" the problem (therapy means "treatment" or "remediation" in Greek.) I usually view my job as helping people to make deep structural changes, so I tend to refer to my work as psychotherapy. But I know counselors who do the same kind of work. Always feel free to ask a counselor or therapist to describe what they do, and why they describe their work as counseling or therapy.

What to Ask a Therapist or Counselor

It's perfectly acceptable, and quite a good idea to ask a therapist about their credentials. It's wise to ask these questions in your first telephone call, so that you don't waste an appointment because you end up not feeling they are qualified to help you. And once you meet a therapist or counselor, feel free to ask what other life and work experience or personal healing they have that might be useful in their work with you. Some counselors or therapists may not feel comfortable answering this question, because they may feel it crosses a personal boundary. However, a counselor or therapist should be able to give you non-specific information that gives you some sense of whether you will have a good "fit" with them. (We often call this a good "clinical fit.")

Regardless of how you are referred to a therapist, feel free to ask them about their healing methods. Some therapists may be strictly required to offer research-based methods only, especially in hospital and university settings. Therapists in private practice often have a little more freedom to combine research-based methods that have a track record of clinical effectiveness, along with emerging methods and technologies that are less established. When you do ask therapists in agencies and in private practice about their healing methods, you'll often find that they are "eclectic," that is, that they combine methodologies. In my work, I often combine, or choose from CBT (cognitive-behavioral therapy), clinical hypnosis, EMDR, systems therapy for individual and family therapy, Imago therapy for couples, energy methods (such as TFT, Reiki, and TAT), and spiritual methods. (In the next section I will tell you about the three of these that are the most "tried and true" and the most commonly available.) Some therapists are purists and use only one method, and find that very effective. What's important is that a therapist or counselor be able to tell you why they're using what they're using, how it works, and what you should be able to expect out of the process. And frankly, some people don't care *what* their therapist uses, as long as it works!

If you are interested, however, feel free to ask for an explanation of:

- A therapist's methods
- Where and/or how they got their training, and how much experience they have with their method(s)
- If the method(s) are approved or accredited, and likely to be covered by an insurer
- How long the process can take
- Risks or side-effects, if any
- What it costs and whether they have a sliding scale
- Their confidentiality policy.

Now I want to list for you some of the best-known and best-researched therapies, some of the common problems that they are particularly good at treating, and considerations you should keep in mind as you go. This list is not exhaustive; rather it focuses on methods that are commonly available and have reasonable records of effectiveness. My intention is to give you a starting point for asking questions, so that you can make your own decision about what feels right for you.

The Big Three

Clinical Hypnosis, Cognitive Behavioral Therapy, and EMDR are arguably the best-researched and most widely used therapy modalities available today. They are often used by themselves, or in combination with several of the other methods listed in the history box a few pages ago. Each of these therapies works well for a variety of problems, and in my experience, each of them excels for some specific problems. Here's a bit of information about these therapies:

1) You Are Getting Very Sleepy...

Everyone has the capacity to shift into natural trance states. In fact, you may shift into and out of mini trance states throughout the day and not even realize it. Have you ever driven home and not remembered the drive? Have you ever watched a movie and completely lost track of time? Well, trance states can be induced in other ways too, and they can be focused to produce deep healing in mind and body. Clinical Hypnosis makes use of your brain's natural ability to shift into trance states, and actually does it *without* you having to go to sleep. It is approved by the American Psychological Association and the American Medical Association. It has a long track record treating problem habits such as smoking, over-eating and even hair-pulling (which is called "trichotillomania"), can be used to strengthen resources such as study habits, learning and concentration, self-esteem, public-speaking skills, and is used widely to promote comfort and healing in medical and dental procedures, to name just a few of its applications. (It also *does* work very well for insomnia, and after that kind of hypnosis, you may very well get sleepy...) Clinical Hypnosis is also a well-established method for treating Dissociative Identity Disorder, which as I mentioned earlier, is a problem that develops for some people after sustained or particularly invasive trauma. Hypnosis helps those folks to "integrate," or bring together the parts of their consciousness that may have partitioned themselves off while trying to keep trauma memory in storage.

However, I have come to prefer EMDR to clinical hypnosis for healing other types of trauma and childhood wounds, because EMDR seems to work at a cellular level that produces measurable, lasting results, and there is substantial research to back up that impression.

There's a form of clinical hypnosis called "Ericksonian" hypnotherapy, as it was developed by Dr. Milton Erickson. It is an informal form of hypnosis that accomplishes the same things as formal hypnosis, and it's often used in combination with formal hypnosis and with other forms of therapy, including Cognitive Behavioral Therapy and EMDR.

Not all people who offer hypnosis are trained in clinical hypnotherapy, nor are they necessarily registered or licensed. It is very important that you work with a properly trained and licensed professional when using hypnosis.

Check out the Appendix for a link to the American Society of Clinical Hypnosis, where you can get lots of great information, including a list of practitioners in your area.

2) You're Smarter than you Think...

Cognitive Behavioral Therapy will get your thoughts, feelings and behaviors cooperating, so that you can feel better and start making smart choices. It is a well-established therapy approved by the American Psychological Association, and has an extremely strong record in treating many of the mood disorders, including many forms of depression and anxiety. It can be used by itself for these problems, but in some cases is more effective when it is combined with medication in certain people. CBT is also very effective for helping people discover how their self-talk is linked to their feelings and behavioral choices in many areas of life, and in assisting them to change patterns and outcomes that have been keeping them stuck. However, it has been my experience that CBT alone is not the most effective tool to heal some types of History. Some people cannot make good use of CBT if they have undetected or unresolved Brain and Body issues or underlying childhood wounds or adult traumas which need healing. In those cases I make sure the Brain and Body is stabilized, address the History with EMDR, and then I find that people can make use of, and hold on to new ways of thinking, managing their feelings, and making behavioral choices (so that they don't repeat their History!)

In Chapter Three I'll teach you a CBT method to help you get started on changing your energy field inside and out, even if you still need to plug in a few Brain and Body supports, and even if you need to get your History healed too. And as you'll see, if you find self-talk strategies too hard to use, that may be a sign that you still need some healing in the First and Second Domains — Brain and Body, and your History.

See the links in the Appendix to the websites of the American Psychological Association and to the National Association of Cognitive-Behavioral Therapists.

3) *Your Brain is its Own Healer...*

EMDR was discovered by accident in the late 1980s, and it has turned out to be a "power therapy" because it quickly goes deep and heals many issues right to the roots. It was originally called Eye Movement Desensitization and Reprocessing, because it was thought that controlled eye movements were required to facilitate the process of healing negative experience. However, over the years, it was learned that the method also works other ways. Controlled exposure to rapidly alternating auditory tones or a tactile stimulus such as hand buzzers or even gentle tapping will help the brain shift into "healing gear" and trigger deep change. In EMDR, the individual is assisted to focus on an experience which needs healing, is asked to identify and rate the feelings and thoughts they notice, and to locate and rate any physical sensations they notice when they are thinking about the negative experience. They are then exposed to short "sets" of the sensory stimulus (eye movements, sound, buzzing or tapping) and the memory begins to "reprocess."

You will remember that earlier in this chapter, we looked at how memory gets stored in the body, and how it can repeat in negative ways if it is unresolved. Well, considerable research has demonstrated that EMDR does an excellent job of resolving negative memory, allowing you to keep your memory of your own experience, but without the negative feelings attached. In other words, it's no longer stuck in your body, having been integrated into your brain in a comfortable way where it will no longer interfere with your life.

EMDR is extremely effective for healing childhood and adult traumas such as abuse, and can go a long way towards healing the effects of neglect and abandonment, including attachment wounds. (Attachment wounds often require additional kinds of intervention, supports, new learning experiences, and learning of self-management skills.) EMDR is also superb for healing both old and recent traumas. It's used around the world for healing after vehicular accidents and natural disasters, for victims of war, for witnesses and victims of crime and violence, and as an adjunct in treating addictions, fetal alcohol syndrome, and even medical traumas such as phantom limb pain. It has been used with great success with combat survivors and with professionals traumatized in the line of duty, such as police and fire fighters, and emergency medical responders. The list of its uses is long, and growing, since trained EMDR clinicians all over the world continue to experiment with applications of it for a wide variety of mental health issues.

I've used it in my practice for 14 years, treating most of the above-identified kinds of problems, and would say that its effects are profound. I've developed a specific model for EMDR, called the Strategic Developmental Model for EMDR, in which I typically heal people's Histories from early life onward, so that they have a comprehensively healed "foundation" upon which to establish a healthier, happier life.

EMDR is approved by the American Psychological Association as a method for treating trauma. It is important to ensure that your therapist received proper training from an accredited training institute such as the EMDR Institute. For more information and reading resources, see links in the Appendix to websites for the EMDR Institute and the EMDR International Association.

Other Individual Therapies

A number of the other therapies which I listed in the history box a few pages back are widely available. Many of them are not supported by well-controlled research, but have long been respected in specific cultures or for use with particular problems. Therapies that are not well-supported by research are often not covered by insurance providers and health care plans, but because there is a growing respect for alternative practices, many wellness plans and health spending accounts allow individuals to choose alternative procedures as their main approach to a mental health issue, or as an adjunct to treatment through more established methods. If you are considering methods that are considered outside of the mainstream of mental health practice, make sure you ask all the same questions that you would of any therapist. Also, if you want to use alternative methods in conjunction with more established forms of therapy, be sure to let your therapist know, so that he or she can pace or structure your therapy to "dovetail" comfortably (and efficiently and affordably) with your alternative choice or choices.

For example, if a client has already started with a naturopath, nutritionist or dietician before they see me, then I often spend less time addressing Brain and Body issues (or it helps me zero in on persistent symptoms which have not yet responded to those therapies.) And if a client wants to use Reiki, accupressure, cranio-sacral therapy, Healing Touch or Therapeutic Touch, to name just a few, then we can coordinate what might be the most appropriate point in treatment to do so, so that it supports or enhances what we are doing, rather than masks or interferes with our results. See the links in the Appendix for more information about these alternative therapies.

Couple Therapy

If one of the ways you are "wearing" your baggage is by finding yourself in unsuccessful couple relationships, or if you are in a high conflict or low intimacy relationship, or if you are struggling with your parenting role and/or conflicting with your partner about parenting issues, you would be wise to get assistance as a couple. The timing of couple therapy is an interesting thing — some people are ready for it without any other forms of individual healing, and some people are still stuck with limbic wounds, so that doing therapy with them is like trying to referee a pair of hurting (and warring) kids! (not surprising if you remember I mentioned that you can get stuck at a particular age of your development if you have significant wounding from that stage of your life.) If that's what I see, then I tend to do some individual healing with people before we make use of couple processes. Sometimes that involves simply sorting out some Brain and Body issues that leave one or the other person highly vulnerable and/or reactive, or it may involve doing some EMDR to heal underlying trauma so that the trauma does not get reactivated in the couple relationship. (For example, if you were abused by a female, you may find yourself very reactive to certain behaviors of your girlfriend or wife, and healing the *original* wound speeds up healing of the couple relationship.)

There are lots of couple therapy models, but the most important thing to look for is for a therapist with strong credentials and with a professional affiliation that supports their learning and practice. The American Association for Marriage and Family Therapy is one such body that has training programs and certifies many practitioners. Look for the link to their website in the Appendix, where you will find listings for couple therapists in your area.

As with individual therapists and counselors, some marriage and family counselors are "purists" who practice only one main model, and many are eclectic, combining techniques from any of the following models: psychoanalytic, object relations, ego analytic, behavioral, integrative behavioral, cognitive behavioral, emotionally focused or structural strategic. (Whew!)

Fortunately, you don't have to know what any of those models are. One of the best ways to choose a therapist, apart from checking out their credentials and talking to them, is word-of-mouth reputation. People who are satisfied with the help they got will often tell their friends, so pay attention to your friends who are satisfied consumers!

COUPLE THERAPY THAT WORKS

If your couple relationships just don't provide satisfaction, there is help. Imago Relationship Therapy is the couple therapy model I most often use and recommend. It was developed by Dr. Harville Hendrix and his wife Helen LaKelly Hunt in the 1980s, and it is today used around the world. The "Imago" (which is Latin for "image") is the unconscious image of a partner that we carry around inside us, strongly influencing the way we do relationships. Imago therapy is a very practical way to get conscious of how each person's internal relationship "template" or model is influencing them in the relationship, and to create a conscious partnership with deeper intimacy and more effective problem-solving skills. Some of the reasons I like Imago are that it is clearly structured, very efficient, very safe and balanced, it gets to the roots of the problem very quickly, and it teaches easy to learn skills that will last a lifetime. I've also found that it can be used with any two people who are in a relationship, such as two siblings or a mother and daughter. I've also used it for whole families. For more information, and to find a therapist in your area, check out the links in the Appendix. And by the way, if Imago sounds familiar to you, it's probably because it has been featured many times on the Oprah Winfrey show.

It's just about time to check in with Julie again. Before we do, I'd like to share the stories of a couple of folks who got unstuck through healing in the Second Domain by resolving their History. Ed healed major trauma that had kept him stuck for years, with the help of EMDR. Cheryl got unstuck primarily with EMDR on her History, but she also got a bit of help in the other Domains — her self-talk and her spiritual tools.

Prison Hostage! — Ed's Story

Ed was a 44 year old prison guard who was referred to me because he was really stuck. A year earlier, rioting prisoners had stormed the control room where Ed was working, took him and a number of other guards hostage, and held them for hours, threatening them with weapons and abusing them until they were rescued by tactical forces. Naturally, Ed ended up with Post Traumatic Stress Disorder and a year later his life wasn't moving forward at all. He had depression, anxiety, insomnia and anger, he was unable to work, and he was spinning his wheels at home. He had a very concerned wife who had taken on the role of dealing with the bureaucracy that decided what services he was eligible for and whether he could go back to work. Ed had become dependent, and he said he was scared. He appeared timid, walked with a stoop, and really came across as though he was already an old man.

I already knew EMDR would be hugely effective for healing Ed's trauma, but I knew that before I went there, I needed to check out the other Domains of Healing to make sure that nothing else would keep him stuck.

Ed was on some suitable medications for depression, anxiety and insomnia, but it's not uncommon to find them inadequate for a person with PTSD. In fact, medication not really helping offers a good clue that a person needs to heal their History. Since Ed had a suitable diet, and good medical supervision, further Brain and Body interventions were not likely to make a substantial difference. And since it is common for a person with unresolved trauma to have self-talk full of fear, pessimism and defeat, simply doing CBT with Ed wasn't likely to help much either, because he needed to heal his trauma first. So, since resolving his History would be imperative, it was important to get a comprehensive History to make sure his healing would be thorough.

And when we looked deeper at Ed's History, there were red flags waving all over the place!

Turns out, Ed had a big attachment wound: he had had repeated experiences of rejection by both parents, and had been physically abused by them. His relationship template had therefore propelled him for many years to choose partners who mistreated him. Later he chose a more motherly figure, as a reparative way of fulfilling the need for a mother figure.

And most surprising of all, it turned out that several years earlier, Ed had been held hostage in another prison riot and never got any treatment! So he had worked for several years with PTSD! No wonder, when you consider that his early life experience had taught him to suffer and endure (that was his unconscious self-talk.) And his life experience had also taught him to be somewhat dependent upon the decisions of those more powerful than him, so a part of Ed was stuck in his own development, and he never had really had a chance to fully be the man he could be.

So here's what we did: Over the course of a few months, we did EMDR on every major part of Ed's life where he had been mistreated, ending in the hostage incidents. As the weeks went by, Ed healed and sort of "grew up" into his full adult self. He began to voice his joy about unloading his baggage, he began to express himself, and he even began to walk tall, no longer stooped over. He no longer carried an impotent anger at those whom he felt should have protected him; rather he developed an assertiveness about what his future would look like. When we re-examined his traumas, he was no longer triggered by them — at all. (That's one of the best things about EMDR — it is so thorough.) We re-examined his self-talk, and found we did not have to do any CBT, as his self-talk had begun changing spontaneously as his traumas resolved. His sleep improved, his anxiety waned, his depression lifted, and so he was able to titrate off his medications.

He experienced himself as a more effective parent, and he was even able to go to work. Through a simple but thorough healing of only his History, Ed was unstuck!

Often, a person's healing in the Second Domain involves using EMDR to resolve their History, but cognitive and spiritual tools end up playing an important supporting role in getting them unstuck. Cheryl is a great example of this kind of healing:

Street Kid: Cheryl's Story

You wouldn't know Cheryl had been a street kid. Here she was, all grown up, bright and beautiful, in a loving relationship, educated and working in a seniors' center. But when Cheryl came to her first appointment, she described the stuck place she was in: Anxious about her health, not sleeping well, aware of perfectionist and control behaviors, stressed by some of the dynamics in her workplace, not feeling self-confidence, not even feeling good about her name, and not having been comfortable enough to have sex for many months. She had a pretty strong idea that it was her History that was keeping her stuck, and she'd sought counseling previously, but hadn't had any resolution. So by now you can likely guess what we did. We examined her First Domain — Brain and Body, and found that although she had some physical ailments and concerns, she practiced good self-care, had a good diet, was not on any inappropriate medications, and was receiving competent medical care. A bit later, as you'll see, we would add in a very helpful nutritional supplement.

Then we looked at the Second Domain, and there were glaringly obvious traumas that had never been healed. Cheryl had an attachment wound, resulting from major rejection by her mother when she was a child. Her father had been an alcoholic, her mother had been highly self-focused (remember narcissism?), and they had had an ugly split when Cheryl was in grade school, exposing her to an unhealthy adult relationship model. Cheryl had left home as a young teenager due to mom's cruelty, and without resources or options had ended up on the streets, relying on older guys to provide for her, often in exchange for sexual favors that Cheryl loathed having to provide. She was physically abused and threatened, and she was exposed to sexually transmitted disease, which left her with a lasting legacy of health concerns. Survivor that she was, she sought help from the straight world, and eventually got off the streets in her late teens, put herself through school, and eventually even went to college.

Cheryl had a huge void inside her where intimacy should have been, and it propelled her to seek a relationship with a man. She cycled through a few learning relationships with men, maturing as she went, and eventually found a wonderful partner who cherished and nurtured her.

But as reparative as that relationship continued to be, Cheryl did not feel at home in her own skin, as she described it. She lacked the confidence to assert herself at work, worried about her physical health, felt shame about the health legacy she carried with her (an STD which she didn't want to identify til much later in our work), felt a lack of sexual desire (no surprise), and was prone to anxiety, and control or perfection behaviors as a way to reduce that anxiety. Cheryl's self-talk was a reflection of her experience: "I'm defective, diseased, tainted, I'm a burden, I'm bothering people, I don't deserve to exist." And she didn't have any spiritual tools that were particularly helpful, so her energy kept her stuck and the Universe didn't feel like a very life-giving source. Her long years of being stuck with the baggage of her history had closed her energy field to some degree, and she had only been able to very carefully let a few safe things in.

She had sent out little of the grateful energy that would easily attract back to her more of what she desired.

So of course we started EMDR, and Cheryl determinedly dug into her past in order to off-load it. She responded steadily, while stopping at each place that her self-shaming self-talk was proving disruptive, allowing us to rationally address the distortions in her beliefs and her self-worth that were undermining her. As her trauma experience and her self-talk healed, Cheryl was able to disclose that the STD she'd been left with was genital herpes. This was a huge step for her, and a very self-empowering one, because it allowed me to tell her about the nutritional supplement L-lysine. (L-lysine is an amino acid which must be in balance in the body with another amino acid called L-arginine. During stress, or with the wrong kind of diet, these amino acids can get out of balance, activating the herpes virus in people who have previously contracted it. Research shows that supplementation with L-lysine can dramatically reduce herpes outbreaks, especially when supported by a diet that is high in L-lysine.) Cheryl began L-lysine and within a couple of months had stopped having outbreaks, for the first time in years.

As we proceeded with EMDR and cognitive work, Cheryl also opened herself to hearing some of the metaphysical information that we'll talk about in Chapter Four. She also decided to watch the movie "The Secret," and realized that she really needed to begin to express gratitude for the good things in her life. As we approached the end of targeting Cheryl's traumas, she began gaining energy and confidence, felt more able to assert herself in her work setting, felt more comfortable with her name, was less worried about her physical health, felt less anxious, and was less controlling or perfectionistic. We knew that Cheryl was close to the end of her healing when she asked for help to get more comfortable with the idea of sexual intimacy with her husband. I set Cheryl and her husband up on a simple behavioral plan, and great, comfortable, fun sex happened spontaneously before they had time to work their way all the way through the behavioral plan!

Cheryl had all four Domains of her life in balance, and she felt great.

At Cheryl's last session she said "I'm inhabiting my skin differently! I am practicing gratitude, I feel celebratory! It's strange, I've lived one way for 32 years, but now I'm going to live this way!"

I hope you're starting to get an idea of what's possible if you've been stuck in your life. It's time to check in on Julie again, and find out more about the strategies that started to change her life.

Healing Julie's History

Julie was sick of the unsupportive people she seemed to attract, the bad relationships with men, the scapegoating that was still directed at her by her family, the financial stress, and the sense that all her hard work kept amounting to more of the same. As I've mentioned, Julie had become like the cartoon character with the cloud of dust over her head, attracting trouble no matter what she did. We had already stabilized Julie in the First Domain — her Brain and Body. But now we knew we'd need to do EMDR on her growing-up experiences, and use cognitive and behavioral tools to change the powerful negative script that ran endlessly in her head (consciously at times, and other times unconsciously.) So we began the process of EMDR, and it helped Julie to unload a lot of the pain she carried from living in her family. Week by week, we worked through the physical abuse, the shaming, the scapegoating, the poverty that taught her the world was not an abundant place. We worked through most of the history of the men who'd drunk too much, taken her for granted, and hurt her physically. The further we went, the less triggered by her past she felt, and the less angry she felt. Julie noticed she was sleeping better and said "I'm noticing I'm happy!"

Before long, Julie met a man she wanted to pursue a relationship with, and because it meant moving away, she ended up not finishing her healing on relationships with men. So guess what happened? Her radar wasn't fully operational, her self-talk couldn't be counted on to tell her the truth, her inner relationship template wasn't fully healed, her boundaries were not self-protective enough, and her energy wasn't fully cleaned up. The man turned out to be abusive, and Julie realized at that point that she needed to return and complete her healing.

You'll hear about how Julie finished her healing in Chapters Three and Four, because changing her world view ended up being the missing piece to her life strategy.

Julie's experience is a perfect lead-in to the question "How can I be sure that my history is healed?" There are some things you need to look for to be sure you won't end up two-steps-forward, one-step-back the way Julie did for a while.

3) How Can I be Sure that My History is Healed?

With the forms of therapy that we have available today, when practiced by well-trained competent therapists, many of the wounds and traumas that can occur in a lifetime can be successfully healed. The exceptions to this, to some degree, are the early-life emotional wounds that result in personality disorders.

CAN PERSONALITY DISORDERS HEAL?

Some things you can change, some things...not so much. We all have *states*, like passing moods for example, and they aren't necessarily a fixed-forever part of us. If we need to change these parts of ourselves, we can, with a little help. We also have *traits*, which are deeper, more enduring aspects of our personalities. These parts of our personalities may be shaped by our upbringing and our heredity. They are harder to change. But if we are generally healthy, we can learn to work around, balance or compensate for the less appealing parts of our personality.

When people are deeply wounded early in their development, they may develop a personality disorder. Their negative personality traits may be deeply fixed, and create much suffering for themselves or others. A personality disorder can be described as "an enduring pattern of inner experience and behavior that deviates markedly from the expectations of the individual's culture, is pervasive and inflexible, has an onset in adolescence or early adulthood, is stable over time, and leads to distress or impairment."[8]

Ten personality disorders have been identified: Paranoid, Schizoid, Schizotypal, Antisocial, Borderline, Histrionic, Narcissistic, Avoidant, Dependent and Obsessive-Compulsive (not to be confused with Obsessive Compulsive Disorder, which is not necessarily "set" and which is amenable to treatment.) Although there is no cure for a personality disorder, there are medications that help to stabilize some personality-disordered people. There are also therapies that can help personality-disordered folks to cope better in the world. For example, Borderline Personality responds quite well to Dialectical Behavior Therapy (DBT for short), which uses cognitive-behavioral strategies to help borderline folks to better self-regulate and stay grounded to reality. Check out the links in the Appendix for more information about coping with Borderline Personality, and for information about DBT.

Fortunately for most people, the human brain is pretty resilient to many kinds of experience. With positive and loving experiences in our lives, as well as appropriate therapy when needed, we can not only recover well from trouble, but we can even transform that trouble into wisdom and new strength.

How do you know your experience has healed? The same way some people know that they don't need therapy at all:

- Your trauma memories don't repeat. When you think of your bad experience, it feels kind of faded and distant, or inactive and finished. You can comfortably think of it, but have not much need to. You have perspective about its place or meaning in your life, but feel free to move on and live well, confident that your trauma memory will not interfere.

- You don't use drugs, alcohol, food, sex, gambling, shopping, spending or the Internet to numb or comfort yourself, or to block out memories.

- Your self-talk is generally optimistic, and even on difficult days, you can get control of any pessimistic or negative thoughts, guide yourself to effective behaviors, and focus on solutions.

- You don't hold resentments or keep score.

- You can handle anger, frustration and disappointment in healthy ways.

- You can ask for help when you need it, and you can offer help without being asked.

- Your inner relationship template attracts healthy and positive people into your life.

- Your boundaries are neither too weak, nor too rigid, just flexible enough to help you define yourself and your space,

8 American Psychiatric Association, 2000. *DSM — IV-TR: Diagnostic and Statistical Manual of Mental Disorders*, 4th edition. Washington: American Psychiatric Association.

protect you when needed, allow in resources and supports, and allow you to reach out and connect to the world you live in.

- Your behaviors are congruent with your values. You don't behave in ways that leave you feeling regret, shame or confusion, or if you slip, you take responsibility.

- You have meaningful pursuits in your life, whether related to family life, work, education, volunteer activities, or recreation.

If these things are missing from your life, it would be wise for you to explore whether you have something that needs healing. It could be that there is a Brain and Body issue, or an unresolved History issue that needs attention. Competent counseling or therapy should absolutely get you unstuck. But if after balancing your Brain and Body, and healing your History, you find you cycle back into old patterns, there are a couple of areas that you should take a closer look at: Your Self-Talk and Your Connection to the Universe. The Third and Fourth Domains likely hold the clues to the transformation you are seeking.

Let's look for those clues next in the Third Domain …

Chapter Three

I'M AT WAR WITH MYSELF!

The Third Domain of Healing:
Your Self-Talk versus Your Inner Voice

*"As human beings, our greatness lies
not so much in being able to remake the world ...
as in being able to remake ourselves."*
Mahatma Gandhi

MAHATMA GANDHI KNEW a secret. Without wealth or privilege, with only the clothing on his back and a determination born out of oppression, he overthrew a powerful political system. Mahatma Gandhi, the great reformer of India, knew something about the power of belief and thought. He used the only tools available to him — his understanding that as a human being he was innately powerful because he could use his thoughts by directing them as intention. He understood that his thoughts and his intention sent a signal to larger forces in the Universe, and that if he behaved in ways designed to live out his thoughts and intention, miracles would happen.

A couple of generations later, Nelson Mandela used the same principles to oust the oppressive political regime in South Africa.

Neither of these men would have said that there was anything special about them. In fact, they simply used various forms of determined thought (including meditation and prayer) to stay focused on their goals, and to catalyze the innate power of average people all around them. They knew that thoughts gently but firmly directed at a goal, as consistently as possible, would bring a harvest. They didn't worry whether they could immediately see the outcome; they just knew that if they set their intention, managed their thoughts to support their intention, and behaved as consistently as they could with their desired outcome, the harvest would come.

You are no different from famous reformers like Gandhi and Mandela. Really! Your thoughts are just as powerful. In fact, because you are so powerful, if your thoughts up to this point in your life have been pessimistic, resigned, negative or similarly "low grade," then you have probably done a pretty good job of attracting conditions that create more of the same. You see, you are both a magnet and a radio transmitter. The thoughts in your brain, both unconscious and conscious, do more than just run your system. Besides getting you from point A to point B, they radiate out to the molecular universe in which you live, and attract back information on the same frequency! This makes you an incredibly powerful being. And *that* is why this book is all about healing — because if you are circulating and radiating out the thoughts of an unhealed life, you are a magnet for everything you don't want, and you are repelling everything you *do* want.

I want to help you fix this. I want to help you use your thoughts like my client Justin, a broke and unemployed musician, who with no prior practice or training, with no other spiritual or metaphysical tools other than what I gave him in one session, went home from our session, set his intention and manifested a new free keyboard and a new free set of tires in just a few days. I want to help you do what Julie did, as you'll later hear more about: bankrupt and lonely, with no prior training and no other spiritual or metaphysical tools other than what I gave her in one session, went home, set her intention and in 16 days manifested a discharge from bankruptcy, a new apartment, a new job and a free trip to Las Vegas (and a free vacuum cleaner and a date with a guy she really liked a couple of weeks later!)[9]

Why are these things possible? For the same reason that Gandhi and Mandela overcame the odds — because there is a whole quantum universe lined up at your disposal, that's why! The physics are truly set up to serve you, and even a modicum of intention, even a small amount of directing your thoughts and cognitions can produce what you desire.

QUANTUM SURPRISES ABOUT YOUR THOUGHTS

Thought produces outcomes! It does so because it is energy. Thought vibrates within the energy field in which you live, affects things around you and produces outcomes. And when thought is directed through intention in a laboratory setting, or through the ambience of prayer and meditation, or through a wide variety of focused healing practices, including traditional and cultural practices, *the evidence is clear that directed thought (i.e. intention) influences outcomes.*

Did you know that human thoughts, when directed with only gentle intention, can influence the activities of tiny live organisms like bacteria and yeast or human cells and enzymes? Thought directed with intention can also directly affect larger life forms such as plants, ants, chicks, mice and rats, cats and dogs. Thought can even influence certain behaviors and brain rhythms of other people! These findings come from controlled research with ordinary people who exercised ordinary mental powers.[9]

What produced these results for these people was their *intention*, particularly if their intention was *gentle*. And a close look at the studies in which people "willed" these things to happen shows that the more the research

---

9 Braud, W. and M. Schlitz. (1983). "Psychokinetic influence on electrodermal activity," *Journal of Parapsychology.* 47: 95-119.

subjects appeared to relate to the living object that they were trying to influence, the more successful they were in using their intention to affect outcome. And the more they viewed living beings as all inter-connected, the more able they were to influence the living subjects they focused on.[10]

Numerous controlled studies at respected institutions have also demonstrated that prayer, which is a form of focused intention, influences agricultural, biological, and medical outcomes, producing higher crop yields, more stabilized biological systems, and measurable health improvements in human beings. And these studies aren't just recent ones. These results have been rolling in over a number of decades, in scientific settings all over the world, and in cooperative studies between scientific settings and people from a variety of religious, spiritual and psychic backgrounds.

And it turns out that human thought can produce not only outwardly-directed and outwardly-measurable outcomes, but it can *interfere* with *incoming* intentions of others as well! William Braud, the American scientist mentioned earlier, conducted controlled experiments in which some individuals were instructed to use thought to shield themselves from the effects of intentional thought being directed at them by others, while others were not. The unshielded participants ended up with significantly elevated biological activity, as measured by their electrodermal (skin) responses, while those who had shielded themselves mentally or psychologically showed significantly fewer physical effects.[11,12]

So it's clear: Thought produces outcomes.

10 McTaggart, L. 2002. *The Field*. New York: HarperCollins.

11 Braud, W. "Blocking/shielding psychic functioning through psychological and psychic techniques: a report of three preliminary studies," in R. White and I. Solfvin (eds.), *Research in Parapsychology*, 1984,42-44.

12 Braud, W. "Implications and applications of laboratory psi findings," *European Journal of Parapsychology*, 1990-1991; 8: 57-65.

Your Self-Talk versus Your Inner Voice

Your brain is constantly making meaning, whether you know it or not, and whether you want it to or not. That's right. To be able to use your intention effectively, you are going to need strategies to overcome the fact that with you or without you, your brain is wired to automatically make meanings! That's right: as soon as the language and memory functions of your brain come on-line in early childhood, your brain develops systems for categorizing, cross-referencing, and imprinting with meaning the details of your experience. Whether you want it to or not, your brain is wired to create a story, a narrative about everything you experience. Your left brain takes the social and emotional information that comes in through your right brain, and makes up a story about it — true or false. That's right — what is so amazing about your brain is that even if parts of it aren't working, even if your brain is damaged, it will create a story at any time, based on any available (or even incomplete) information. And the story may be complete fiction! So the script in your head can run whether you're conscious of it or not, be completely false, and interfere with your true intentions.

There is a famous story about a brilliant man whose brain just wouldn't stop making up meanings, even after he experienced some brain damage. He served as an Associate Justice on the U.S. Supreme Court, and in 1974 he suffered a massive stroke in the right hemisphere of his brain. This meant that his ability to correctly interpret social cues was impaired, and that he was essentially unable to incorporate external cues about what was correct or truthful into the meaning-making activities of his left brain. He began to deny the cause of his paralysis, and to claim that he was the Chief Justice, rather than an Associate, or later, a former Associate. After these behaviors persisted, he of course had to leave the Supreme Court, and even then he resisted, asking that a tenth seat be placed for him at the Justices' bench. He didn't "get" that the meaning-making capabilities of his left brain were compromised by a lack of accurate right-brain information, so this formerly brilliant jurist (and arbiter of truth!) just went ahead and made up stories about his condition to suit his left brain's need for a narrative![3] Most of us will not suffer brain damage in our lives, and will retain the great privilege and luxury of being able to be conscious of our own meaning-making processes, and to intervene in them.

> And by the way, that's why the correct full name of our species isn't "homo sapiens ," which means "wise human;" rather it is "homo sapiens sapiens," which means "wise human who *knows* s/he is wise." It is what we do with this capacity to be aware of our own thought processes that determines whether we will construct a great and expansive life or only a shadow of the life we really dream of.

13 Gardner, H., Brownell, H.H., Wapner, W., Michelow, D. 1983. "Missing the Point: The role of the right hemisphere in the processing of complex linguistic materials." In Perceman, E., ed. *Cognitive Processing in the Right Hemisphere.* New York: Academic Press.

In the Introduction to this book, I mentioned that our self-talk is like a script or story that runs in our head, that it can get "anchored" in our brains, and if it is negative, can undermine us in powerful ways. To the extent that our consciousness allows, brain damaged or not, we need to stay aware of the meanings our brain is making up! To be unaware is to risk living a life that is scripted outside our consciousness, one that is potentially completely at odds with what we really want and who we really want to be.

I've also mentioned that when negative self-talk is entrenched and repeating like a circuit, it can make it difficult to hear our Inner Voice, which is the source of wisdom and higher guidance which we all possess. So let's talk for a minute about the Inner Voice, since everything we do to heal and clean up self-talk is designed to allow that Inner Voice to be heard. What exactly is your Inner Voice? Well, experience suggests that your Inner Voice is a source of truth about you, about who you are or were meant to be, about your deepest gifts and talents, about the path you would be happiest taking, about the meaning of your life. Many people hear their Inner Voice early in life, but are taught to doubt it or put it down. The gifts they possess are not valued by the family they were born into, or the path they dream of is one that seems impossible at their socio-economic level. Some people's dreams seem foreign or threatening to their loved ones, or the meaning and limits of life appear to already be defined or dictated by culture or gender. Eventually it becomes too painful to hear the authentic Inner Voice, so in time it is not listened to. Sometimes the struggle for survival is all-consuming: abuse, abandonment, ill health, lack of education, etc. rear their ugly heads, and listening to the promptings of an inner source of wisdom becomes a luxury that can't be afforded. Instead, painful histories and wounding experiences get converted into self-talk by our meaning-making brains, and so a negative world-view is kept alive and *that* is what gets heard. In time, the Inner Voice becomes so hard to hear that a person can forget it was ever there.

Even when you no longer hear your Inner Voice, in quantum thinking its energy is still within your field. All we need to do is clean up your self-talk so that you can re-connect with it. Fortunately, the Zero Point Field, the endless field of vibrating quantum energy, appears to be a vast storehouse of information, including information which was contained at a previous point in time within the energy field of a biological entity!

For example, in one experiment in which part of a leaf was cut away, the entire energy field of the original leaf showed up when a Kirlian (high voltage) photograph was taken of the damaged leaf! Quantum thinking is that any two subatomic particles (bits of energy) that have co-existed can still communicate with one another even after they are separated. So you *can* re-connect with your wise Inner Voice even if you have shut it off or have not been able to hear it for a long time.

Healing Processes for your Self-Talk

Before we "go big" by enlisting quantum forces in your self-talk processes, let's take a look at some of the tried-and-true healing processes that can make a big difference in cleaning up your inner narrative. The more you know about these things, the better equipped you will be, especially on the days when you need a boost.

Cognitive Behavioral Techniques

Thoughts-are-feelings-are-outcomes. As you may remember from Chapter Two, in the 1950s and 60s therapists started realizing that thinking underlies emotions. It may seem obvious now, but it wasn't then. Psychological and emotional problems were thought to have other origins, and it took time to discover that thinking not only underlies emotions, but that together thoughts and feelings then shape choices and behaviors and **outcomes.**

Thoughts				Choice
Perceptions	⇨	Feelings	⇨	Behaviours
Beliefs				OUTCOMES

There is a little saying in neurobiology: What fires together, wires together!

This means that:

1. because thoughts, perceptions and beliefs lead to certain sets of feelings,

2. and those thoughts and feelings then lead you to certain choices, behaviors and outcomes,

3. they wire together, so the outcomes tend to reinforce the beliefs that got you there, and a cycle is born: your thoughts lead to outcomes, your outcomes convince you that your thoughts were correct, and around and around it goes. You become a prisoner of your own thought, feeling and behaving cycle, always producing the same kinds of outcomes.

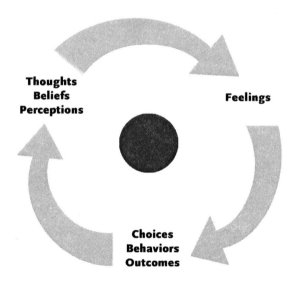

Thoughts
Beliefs
Perceptions

Feelings

Choices
Behaviors
Outcomes

Experience tells us that in order to change feelings and outcomes, we have to change the thoughts, perceptions and beliefs. In order to have a life that *feels* better, we have to start changing the inner script or story *first*. Experts agree that there are a few simple steps to break out of a negative thinking-feeling-outcome cycle:

1. Tune in to your self-talk (check in on it frequently!)

2. Do (almost) anything you need to do to shut off/shut down negative self-talk

3. Be willing to substitute new positive thoughts

4. Be willing to rehearse and practice new behaviors, even *before* your feelings change (kind of like "fake it til you make it.")

So let's take a closer look at these steps, and I'll share with you the strategies that I've seen work the best for a wide variety of people who struggled with fear, anxiety, depression, anger, addictions, and/or compulsive behaviors, to name just a few:

Step One: Tune in to your Self-Talk

Be aware that you have at least two levels of self-talk going. On the surface you've got **thoughts** like "I have to get milk on the way home," "I hope that guy doesn't drive into my lane!" "I wish my boss would quit dumping stuff on my desk," "I wonder if my partner will be in a better mood tonight," "s/he can be such a jerk sometimes," "I don't know why I bother," "maybe I'll just ignore him/her tonight," "how did I get stuck in this relationship?" "I'm sick of this, I deserve better," etc. So when you get home and your partner hasn't started dinner like they were supposed to, your **perception** is going to be something like "s/he deliberately did this to annoy me," and it's going to reinforce your **belief** that "s/he doesn't care about this relationship." This is very naturally (and speedily!) going to lead to **feelings** like anger, frustration, maybe sadness or resignation or powerlessness, and if not managed, can lead to **behaviors** and **choices** such as yelling, slamming pots, giving the cold shoulder, criticizing, blaming, and maybe having a few too many glasses of wine to unwind, or eating half the tub of ice cream at 10 pm because you need a boost, none of which solves the problem, and all of which leads to more anger, frustration, and now guilt about your weight. So the **thoughts** get louder and more entrenched: "I can *never* count on him/her to help me," "it's always going to be this way," "why me?"

You can see how *that* cycle could go on forever, getting worse each time around. Well, before we look at what to do with those thoughts and feelings, it's important for you to know about the deeper level of self-talk that is going on. If you take a look at the original set of thoughts about the other driver, the boss, the relationship, there's a theme running through it: powerlessness. And when we dig a little deeper, what we often find is an *older*, quieter, more anchored set of beliefs that keep playing, a set of beliefs that came out of your earlier life experiences of powerlessness, of not being heard or cared for. Without realizing it, you've been walking around believing that sooner or later, you'll be hurt, disappointed, and disregarded. And, because your *thoughts create energy*, your real intention (to be loved, supported, respected) can't activate because your defeatist energy is cancelling it out. Consequently, your thoughts attract to you *exactly what you predicted.* You further this cycle by choosing self-soothing or escape options that keep the negative energy circulating, and *you perpetuate your own awful reality.*

If you have earlier life wounds that have contributed to these beliefs, you want to make sure those experiences are healed (EMDR is one of the best ways to heal those kinds of wounds.)

And as you know from Chapter One, if you have unregulated biochemical issues going on that affect your mood states, you must take care of those. But the other thing you can do, all on your own, is to become an observer of your own thinking, and to learn to shut down the negative thoughts before they take on a life of their own. This is an incredibly powerful way to stop the energy from attracting and creating more of the same. And I need to emphasize, **you must do this first in order to create good feelings; you don't wait for the good feelings to happen first, because they won't.** You are an incredibly powerful person: you create your reality moment by moment, you co-create with the Universe by choosing how to use your thought-energies and producing certain outcomes. No one is a victim unless he or she hands the Universe that script or story to work with.

What are some of the most common ways people get boxed-in by their own inner thoughts? Well, all the major researchers and clinicians in this field pretty much agree that there are at least ten common habits that you can fall into[14], and they are deadly! They can keep you stuck for a long, long time. They are:

1. **All-or-nothing thinking**: you see things as all one way, or all the other way, with no in-between. Interestingly enough, this "concrete" thinking is what little kids do until their brains are developed enough to see the "gray" or the in-between. So when we're doing this, it can be a clue that we're stuck at a very young life stage (or it just may be that we've got a rigid thought habit that's narrowing our field of vision.)

2. **Over-generalizing**: a clue that you're doing this is if you are using the words "always" or "never." You're taking one negative thing and expanding it to apply to everything else, which immediately limits the accuracy and possibilities within your view.

3. **Personalizing or blaming**: you either take the blame for everything that appears to go wrong, or you heap the blame onto someone else. This is really just another form of black-and-white thinking.

4. **Labeling**: once you or someone else make a mistake, you lump yourself or that person into a locked-in category of idiot/jerk/stupid/loser, and so it's hard to see past the label to the complexities and possibilities in the situation. (More black-and white thinking.)

5. **Magnifying**: you let everything loom larger in your view of reality than it really is (kind of like Alice through the Looking Glass, only not as much fun.)

6. **Mental filters**: you decide that this is the way it is, and so any information gets filtered through your firmly held certainty (or prejudice) and so it gets hard to hear new

---

14 Burns, D. 1980. *Feeling Good*. New York: William Morrow.

information. For example, you believe that authority figures don't listen to you, and so that becomes your experience no matter who the authority figure is.

7. **Shoulds**: you allow to operate in you some great moral judge who decides what should or shouldn't be, and everything that doesn't meet that standard by you or anyone else is reason for contempt or self-blame. Where did that Judge come from? Sometimes it's presence is a clue that you have some healing to do, since the Judge is often what we call a "parental introject" which means that you may have experienced that judging from your own parent, and now you've taken on that role within yourself.

8. **Discounting the positive**: you're afraid to believe things can be different, and so you don't want to invest any hope when something positive does happen, and therefore you just discount it as though it's just a temporary condition that can't possibly last or repeat.

9. **Emotional reasoning**: you distort your experience by allowing your current feeling to be your source of logic: "I feel lonely, I'll probably be alone forever."

10. **Leaping to conclusions**: without allowing yourself to see evidence to the contrary, or without allowing yourself to wait to see what's possible, you "protect" yourself by deciding that the conclusion will be negative, and so you operate as though the outcome has already happened. This ensures that the negative energy from that thought will perpetuate your bad experience, and so you actually prove your own case.

Whatever you believe will be true for you.

Watch Out for the Lies We Tell Ourselves

There are four very common kinds of thinking distortions or excuses that go on inside the heads of people who have a bad habit or behavior or addiction that they are not ready to face: minimizing, rationalizing, justifying and denying. These are four ways to keep yourself from facing the truth about your own behavior, and they can help you stay stuck for years. They can also contribute to you eventually paying a very high price for your behavior. Lots of my clients have come to see me after serving a criminal sentence because they kept using these four types of excuses to enable their behavior, and some of them kept using these excuses even after they were incarcerated, so they were turned down for early parole. Others kept using these excuses, and although they did get out, they repeated their behavior and ended up serving out their sentence back behind bars. Interestingly enough, these four thinking distortions can show up in the rest of us, too, when we really, really, really don't want to have to give something up:

- **Minimizing**: you tell yourself that only having half a brownie won't lead to having the whole thing, so you're not really cheating. You tell yourself one sip isn't going to lead to a whole bottle. You say that the hurtful thing you said to so-and-so wasn't *really* that mean, etc.

- **Rationalizing**: you tell yourself that if you have a brownie tonight, you'll skip something else tomorrow (yeah, right.) You tell yourself that the mean thing you said had to come out sooner or later, and at least they know where you stand.

- **Justifying**: you tell yourself that you *deserve* the brownie because you worked so hard on your taxes, or your front lawn, or the whatever. You tell yourself that having a sip of beer allows you to prove to yourself that you can do it. You tell yourself that you wouldn't have said that mean thing if *she* hadn't started it.

- **Denying**: you say that you didn't really have half a brownie because it was just the loose crumbs in the pan which probably don't add up to half a brownie at all. You say that you smoked a joint but didn't inhale. You say that you didn't say that mean thing at all — it was *her* imagination.

With a little practice, you'll find that when you tune in to your self-talk you can hear some (or many!) of the ten most common distortions or thinking errors. You also will get good at catching one or more of the four lies or excuses that seem to operate when you're not ready to face the truth about something difficult.

So tune in to your self-talk as many times as you need to throughout the day. Listen in on your own brain. Turn up the volume and listen for the two levels of thought that I talked about: what's the surface talk — one of the ten cognitive distortions listed above? If so, you might hear yourself thinking how that guy *will* drive into your lane, or how your boss *won't* be fairer to you, or how your partner *definitely* doesn't want you to be happy. If it's one of the four lies or excuses, you might hear yourself justifying how you *do* deserve such-and-such just this one time.

Then go deeper. Ask yourself "what's the earliest time in my life that I thought this way?" "when else have I thought similar thoughts?" Help yourself see that your thoughts are an expression of *beliefs* you have carried around for a long time, and that it will be necessary to go to war against those deeper beliefs. Decide that you *want* to go to war against those beliefs.

Step Two: Shut Down Your Negative Thoughts

Your negative thoughts are your enemy! Decide that you will do everything in your power to wipe them out. You've already lived according to those beliefs for a long time and where did they get you? What do you have to lose by temporarily suspending them and experimentally operating with a different set of thoughts? You don't have to worry about *believing* some new thoughts, you just have to be willing to substitute them every time you hear the old garbage thinking. You have to be willing to fake it til you make it. The good feelings won't come until you do this. Are you willing to invest in yourself? You have to be if you want to experience something different. ***So set your intention.***

When you have made this decision, you are ready to begin the daily process of dismantling these thought patterns. Here are some tried-and-true ways to wage war on your own destructive thinking:

The Big Smack-Down

The first thing to do, as soon as you become aware of an errant thought, a potentially destructive belief operating, is to smack it down! There are all kinds of ways you can do this. You can say to yourself: "Whoa, that sounds familiar! No way am I going there right now! No way am I letting that thought have any more air-time in my brain! Where has it gotten me? I don't care if it feels true, no way am I investing it with energy or intention, and there's no way I am giving that one any more room to script my future. I need my energy available for other possibilities. And besides, just because I had some experiences that led me to believe that thought is true, doesn't mean I can't open myself to some new possibilities that disprove it. After all, if experience is what taught me to believe that, then deliberately choosing other experience will allow me to develop some different beliefs."

In a minute, we'll talk about what to substitute once you smack down the negative thought, because you must fill up the space with new material (since Nature abhors a vacuum!) But first, here are a few more ways to intervene in your own brain:

Partition Your Mind

As soon as you hear one of the negative thoughts you are prone to, put up a partition, a wall, a barrier straight through the middle of your brain, and push that thought onto the left side of the barrier. It's just like creating a dam or levee — your job in desperate times is to contain unwanted "toxic spill." Use all your intention to keep the thought on that side of your brain. Then start picturing the thought shrinking. That's right, contain it and shrink it. What will help you to do so is to remind yourself that it's just a thought, it has no concrete merit unless you give it merit. If you don't water it, it can't grow. And tell yourself that no way are you giving that thought control. If you were fighting a toxic spill, would you just give in to the spill on the other side of the dam?

As soon as you've done this, praise yourself. Do a good job of praising yourself. Tell yourself, "wow! Even though I am just learning to do this, I have already taken a couple of good steps. I can use my energy to keep doing this til the good stuff starts to kick in." (Because the good stuff *will* kick in when you have done this for a while.)

Understand that your negative thoughts have put down neural pathways in your brain, and those thoughts have become automatic. But every time you shut off those negative thoughts, you are helping those neural pathways to atrophy, to shrink. Your intervention undoes those pathways, and the "new material" that you'll provide to your brain (in a minute) will lay down new neural tracks, that over time will become automatic. So it is really worth the investment of energy. And yes, it is harder at the beginning, but in time your investment of energy pays you back and you can get on with bigger and more fun ways of spending your energy, *because your brain won't be undermining you.* So do this!

Listen to your Body

If you're having trouble hearing your thoughts, then listen to your body and work backwards! Ask yourself: "hmm, what am I noticing in my body right now? Is there any tension anywhere? any tightness, heaviness, a sick feeling? What kind of stuff is going on for me when I have that feeling?" Most people's bodies react in certain ways when they are having certain types of thoughts:

- Fearful thoughts = tension, gut disturbance, heart pounding, breathing shallowly;

- Sad thoughts = heaviness in chest, lump in throat, no energy, shoulders stooped;

- Angry thoughts = tension all over, jaw clamped, elevated heart rate.

Ask yourself, "what might I be sad about? angry about? afraid of? What am I telling myself right now that is feeding those feelings?

Look Around You

What was going on just before you noticed these thoughts? What was going on for the preceding 24 hours? The clues will be there in your life as to what activated your negative script. Most people have certain "trigger" situations that are likely to activate old beliefs and toxic thinking. If the trigger is one you can reasonably avoid, or at least til you have developed some protective skills, stay away from it! After all, do you really have to make that call to your sister late at night when she is likely to be tired and cranky? Do you really have to have the conversation about the credit card bill when your partner is tired, upset or hungry? Do you really have to visit your parents for the long weekend when you know nasty uncle Floyd is going to be there? Do you have to sit in the *kitchen* doing your paperwork when you are really trying to lose weight? Quite often, with a little planning, you can stay out of a trigger situation entirely, or shorten your exposure to it if it was unexpected. *You* have control over whether you stay in a trigger situation.

Step Three: Plug In New Thoughts

Stop right there! As you're reading this, can you feel yourself thinking "I can't do this. It's going to be too hard. My thoughts *are* true. This won't work for *my* life."?

So *Now* is when you're going to start. Right this minute. You're going to listen to the negative script that is running, you're going to shut it down, partition your brain, shrink the thought, praise yourself for taking that step. Do it right now.

Next, you're going to set your intention to get out from under the grip of this kind of brain chatter.

And now, as quickly as possible, you're going to start to fill up the space you've created with some new material. Some of the tried-and-true ways of doing this are:

- **Find however many of the ten thinking distortions you've got running, and one by one, dismantle them**: "No, I'm not *always* wrong. In fact, here are three times in the last week that I was right. And I am learning to live life differently so that I'll be able to recognize just how wise I really am." " No, it's not true that I *never* have any dates. I just haven't had one in a while, and I *intend* to change that." "No, it's not *necessarily* going to turn out badly. I need to wait to see what possibilities exist in this situation. And besides, I am learning to create possibility for myself." "Who says I *should* do that thing? Who says I *shouldn't* have that thing, that I'm not worthy of it? In fact, I am learning to live an abundant life, and I'll be having a lot *more* good things. " "No, I'm *not* a fool just because I didn't see that coming. I am perfectly smart in lots of ways, and I'm allowed to be less than perfect." "Yes I *can* finish this paper in time. Here are three ways I can re-organize my time to make it happen."

- **Find any of the four lies or excuses that might be operating.** Ask yourself: am I trying to minimize the impact, or justify what ends up being a dangerous course of action, or rationalize/make an excuse to myself? Am I denying anything so I can stay comfortable? Am I denying because I'm scared to change? Do I really want to stay stuck like this? I *can* tell myself the truth, I'm strong enough to face it, and I can ask for help with what I see about myself or what I'm afraid of.

You get the drift. As soon as you do this, *you change the energy you give off, you change your energy field, you start to tap into the larger quantum field, to become a magnet for a different outcome.* Don't worry that you can't *feel* the change yet. The Universe is already starting to realign itself for you, and the feedback will show up. There are a few behavioral things that you're going to need to do to back up your talk, (which we'll look at in a minute) and to really tell the Universe you're serious about change. And the good news is that you don't have to know how to do this perfectly. You just have to be willing to put one foot in front of the other, to plant the seeds, and as you'll see, the process will bear fruit. Your willingness to recognize your unhealthy self-talk, shut it down, and start substituting positive thoughts have already served notice to the quantum field that it can organize itself to respond to you differently.

And remember, we talked about how your early life wounds can slow you down in your development. Well, your willingness to shut down your negative self-talk actually helps to move you past your developmental blocks. It actually helps to stretch your emotional muscles, to develop your frustration tolerance and to be more resilient. So just do it, even if you haven't got the reward yet. It's the only way you can find out that it works.

Some more ways to plug in new constructive thoughts include:

- **Remind yourself of what has worked for you in the past**. Make a list on paper if you have to. Be willing to repeat the steps that created even small successes for you before. Ask people you trust for ideas about how they would accomplish a goal or a task, or overcome a doubt or a fear. List all the possible options, break them down into do-able steps, brainstorm strategies to counter any potential obstacles. Find a support buddy, and help each other clean up self-talk (it's often easier with someone else who can look at your life from a different vantage point.) As soon as you do this, you are serving notice to the quantum field that you *intend* to have success.

- **"Play the movie to the end."** This means think through to the conclusion of what the outcome will be if you hold on to the negative thoughts, and compare it to the projected outcome of your deliberately positive thoughts. A lot of the criminals and addicts I have treated find this one particularly effective. They "play the movie to the end" and see that without altering their thoughts, jail or misery will be their outcome, so they realize "what do I have to lose by deliberately substituting healthier thoughts right now?" Anything they do in the direction of change will be better than the outcomes they have previously created. Go ahead and *intend* to have that better outcome. There is incredible power in that decision.

William Murray was a Scot who knew about tough times and big challenges. While a soldier in World War Two, he was taken captive and spent three years in prisoner of war camps in Europe. During his imprisonment, he occupied himself by writing a book (on toilet paper since that was all that was available), had it destroyed by the Gestapo, and began it all over again. He lived, barely, through a near starvation diet. Upon his release, in spite of the physical debilitation he had experienced, he rebuilt his strength and returned to his passion of high-altitude climbing, and later became a campaigner to protect wilderness areas. Murray continued to write, and eventually penned a passage which would be quoted the world over. It is in these words that he explains what life taught him about the secret of survival and the momentous power of intention:

*"Until one is committed, there is hesitancy, the chance to draw back, always ineffectiveness. Concerning all acts of initiative (and creation), there is one elementary truth, the ignorance of which kills countless ideas and splendid plans: that the moment one **definitely commits oneself** then providence moves too. A whole stream of events issues from the decision, raising in one's favor all manner of unforeseen incidents, meetings and material assistance, which no man could have dreamt would have come his way. I learned a deep respect for one of Goethe's couplets:*

Whatever you can do or dream you can, begin it.
Boldness has genius, power and magic in it!"[15]

William Murray didn't know how the Universe would align itself to help him, he just knew he had no choice but to set his intention, to commit himself to what he desired. It's the same for you. When you are so boxed in by the limitations of your life, when you are sick enough of what you're living in, you have nothing to lose, and everything to gain by

---

15 Murray, W. H. 1951. *The Scottish Himalayan Expedition*. London: Dent Publ.

committing yourself to change and *taking the steps* to show the Universe you are open for business. So let's look at how you take the steps to get you where you want to go.

Step Four: Practice New Behaviors

If you want something you've never had, you've got to do something you've never done.

(Einstein said you can't keep doing the same thing and expect to get a different result.) So as soon as you've listened in to your automatic negative thinking, taken steps to shut it off, started to substitute new thoughts (however hypothetical they might feel), you are ready to spring into action. This is how you will lay down new neural pathways in your brain, this is how you will change your energy and send a different set of instructions to the quantum field, to the Universe, to the ordinary world around you, that you are intent upon a different outcome.

And let's be clear: this doesn't have to be a long, ponderous process. In fact, you can do the whole thing several times a day, in as little as a minute: what am I thinking? okay, let's get that shut off or partitioned. now, what would be a smarter thought? okay, now what behavior can I enact right this minute to finish breaking out of the cycle?

The easiest way to identify smart new behaviors that are likely to produce different outcomes, is to take a look at the coping strategies that aren't working for you, and *do the opposite.*

George Does the Opposite

There's a very funny Seinfeld episode in which George, dispirited about his life, decides one day to just do the opposite of whatever he would normally do, thinking that maybe it will result in something different. Sitting in the coffee shop with Jerry, he boldly changes his sandwich order, and feels empowered.

Then he notices a beautiful woman sitting some distance away. She glances at him, and in that moment you can hear George's automatic thinking as it plays itself out: No way could that woman be looking at me, no way could I be successful in talking to her, what's the point of even trying? etc, etc. His friends remind him he's decided to "do the opposite," so, taking a chance, George gets up from the booth, walks over to the beautiful woman, and boldly says "Hi, my name is George, I'm unemployed and I live with my parents."

The woman bats her eyelashes at him and says, "Hi George, my name's Victoria. Great to meet you."[16] His "luck" changed, because he made a *choice* to act in a new way.

Make a list of the ineffective feel-better strategies you've typically used in the past, and get ready to do the opposite. For example:

- If your thoughts are "I'll always be lonely, no one ever likes me enough to stick around, what's the point?" then your feelings are probably sadness, loneliness, depression, hopelessness. Your coping strategies are likely to be to stay home and watch TV, eat for comfort, go on the computer. So after you have deliberately pushed the thoughts aside, then as quickly as possible forced yourself to look at why those thoughts don't have to be true, you have to practice some new behaviors to send a signal to the Universe, to the quantum field, that you are preparing the ground for something different to grow. So if you wouldn't ordinarily join something, or ask someone to accompany you to something, you're going to do just that. Yes, I know it feels awkward. But so what? Do you like what you have? What I want to help you get is that your gentle intention to attract something different, *followed by a new behavior*, lays the groundwork and creates an energy re-alignment in the molecular universe. You don't have to know what the new

16 Seinfeld, J. 1994. "The Opposite," *Seinfeld*, season 5, episode 22, aired May 19, 1994.

outcome will look like, you just have to be willing to practice one or more new behaviors, over and over, until you start to get a different result. I am not kidding you about this. It works, but only if you persist with gentle intention and behavioral changes that allow new energy to gradually (or sometimes very quickly) be attracted to you. And that means that you need to keep implementing the new behaviors until they bear fruit. Don't worry if new outcomes don't manifest right away; often you just plant seeds and keep watering them until they grow. And often the Universe will surprise you by having the results manifest in a different way than you were expecting. Just plant the seeds of change and keep watering them — your willingness to do so sets off a powerful chain of events that is not always immediately visible. In the next chapter I will give you lots more information about the quantum physics that make this possible.

- If your thoughts are "I'll never have the kind of job I really want, no one recognizes my abilities, maybe I'm not really very smart after all…" then your feelings are likely to be frustration, maybe anger or hopelessness, and resignation. Your coping behaviors may include isolating yourself at work, not joining with those who you feel don't "get" you, venting about it to your friend or partner, idly looking at job listings, eating or drinking too much at night, etc. So if you want something different, you are going to listen in on those thoughts, deliberately (forcefully if necessary) push them aside, point out to yourself all the reasons that those thoughts don't have to be true, state your intention to attract new conditions, and begin as swiftly as possible to practice some alternative behaviors. It is through your gentle intention and the exercise of your willingness that you will choose someone new to connect with at work, stop venting (because it is perpetuating the energy of your situation and ordering up more of the same), register for a new course or additional training, volunteer for some new experience at work, demonstrate your value by being the "go-to guy or gal" at work, work out in the company gym and talk to people while you are there, and spend your evenings in ways that rest or energize you. You are going to do this *even if you don't feel like it*, because the Universe honors your intention and the efforts you make to attract a new outcome. The beautiful thing is that you don't have to know exactly what the outcome will look like; your efforts will begin to produce new results as long as you persist with gentle intention and the behaviors to back it up. There is a lot of great research that backs this up. Multiple studies of cognitive behavior therapy have demonstrated its ability to change how people feel and behave, and lots of research in quantum physics has demonstrated that the process of intention produces desired outcomes.

REHEARSE YOUR SUCCESS

Behavior Rehearsal is used by successful athletes and achievers of all kinds to help them *feel* how real their success will be. It is a smart strategy that can help you to *prepare* for new behaviors and new results. What you do is set aside some quiet time and envision in detail, moment-by-moment, how you intend to execute the new behavior. Picture yourself taking each step, and feel free to imagine how you will work around any obstacles that may present themselves. With your eyes closed, *live* through each step you are going to take. Feel it in your body, in your muscles. As you do this you are literally laying down new neural pathways that will make the behavior automatic. When athletes do this, the research shows that they actually improve muscle development, even though their mental rehearsal was conducted sitting still!

> Mentally rehearse any new behavior until it feels like a part of your natural repertoire. Then when you implement it in real life, notice anything you might need to add in to your mental rehearsal, so that you feel ready to deal with challenges and obstacles. Highly successful athletes and sales professionals rehearse how they will respond to an obstacle or a "no," so that when it happens it is simply a natural part of the sport or the sale, not an impediment! More importantly, successful athletes and sales people rehearse the win. They envision and feel how it will be to cross the finish line, close the sale, receive the award. It is as important to picture the successful outcome as it is to picture the new behavior, or the handling/shrinking of any obstacles along the way.
>
> When you do this, you are sending a powerful energy out into the world around you, you are "placing your order" and you are attracting the kind of outcomes you desire. Have fun with your rehearsals, picture all kinds of positive outcomes — it gives the Universe lots to work with!

The cognitive-behavioral strategies I've outlined above are just intended to get you started. They are commonly used by people around the world, in therapy and/or on their own, and they work extremely well. They are a great fundamental set of tools to stay in charge of your life. However, if you really want to ramp up to spectacular outcomes and the life you dream of, you will want to add in quantum strategies. We'll look at these very cool tools in the next chapter. Just before we go there, however, I want to tell you about a couple of people who changed their self-talk, overcame self-defeating patterns, and opened up new possibilities for their lives.

Jay is someone who changed the outcomes he kept getting with women, when he changed the way he was thinking about them, and when he followed it up with some new behaviors:

Mr. Nice Guy: Jay's Story

Jay was a successful 34 year old sales professional, as nice as they come. Jay came from a loving family, his Brain and Body were in balance, he didn't have any traumatic experience, and he really looked at life optimistically. He had lots of friends, loved his work, loved to travel. No big complaints, except that he attracted difficult women — beautiful women who couldn't hold their liquor, forgot to mention that they had an STD, stalked him, made threats, and who even claimed pregnancies that mysteriously came and went.

Jay felt stuck. He couldn't figure out what he was doing wrong, and he was frustrated because he really wanted to find a nice partner with whom he had a great fit, and eventually start a family. We knew that in order to help Jay get conscious of how he was producing these bad outcomes with women, we'd have to delve into the Third Domain of Healing, and take a look at the script that was operating in his head. I knew that when we figured out what his automatic thinking was telling him about women, and about dating and relationships, we'd know why he kept setting himself up for heartache.

Jay came from a family in which his dad was a hardworking provider, loving, affectionate, and interested in parenting his kids. His mom was a lighthearted, fun-loving, interactive, artsy woman, who wanted her kids to really savor life. All good. Interestingly, however, when Jay's parents disagreed, the dynamic they'd developed was that the father would lovingly accommodate to his wife's position, and if they disagreed about her money management, for example, Jay's dad would just get a second job and compensate for the shortfall. Jay's mom's happiness was thus sustained, and peace reigned in the household. Jay's dad would make coffee in the morning and take it to his wife in bed, and just generally cherish this playful and vibrant woman. And so it went.

So unbeknownst to Jay, the beliefs he developed at a very early age in relation to women were "just forgive what you disagree with, sacrifice your personal feelings and values, and don't pay too much heed to a red flag." So Jay began his relationship life, and dismissed the warning signs in his first serious relationship. He pretty much ignored his "spider sense," and the behaviors he practiced were various forms of accommodation. When he finally found out from his girlfriend that he had to get tested for an STD, he decided he couldn't carry on in the relationship. He worked his way through two more relationships, giving each one two or more years, as he tried to accommodate to behaviors that were at odds with his values, always hoping for the best. He got pretty good at recognizing when things weren't working, and so he did end things, or thought he did. But when ex-girlfriend number three threw herself on the floor outside his apartment door one night as he entertained a new date, he started to realize that something wasn't working. Still, onward he went into relationship number four.

"We fell in love quickly," Jay told me. And of course, that was the biggest clue of all. What Jay didn't realize was that usually when you "fall in love quickly" (as opposed to feeling very attracted and wanting to pursue it) you *project your fantasy onto the blank screen of the other person's as-yet unknown personality.* What you fall in love with is the projection of an ideal that you have carried around in your head, and when your hormones are pumping and your heart is beating, it is easy to have that image look pretty real. And if, like Jay, you are already wired to overlook the negative and accommodate to the less-than-desirable, then falling in love can be pretty quickly accomplished. (To learn how to slow down a bit and really use the dating process to discover who someone is, read John Gray's *Mars and Venus on a Date.*)

So within the year, because Jay had not really done "due diligence" before getting in pretty deep, he ended up dealing with a woman who couldn't self-regulate, couldn't work through her own distress about things, and who needed high degrees of validation, attention and admiration. These are Borderline Personality traits, and Jay was in over his head. He found himself with some new rationalizations added to his self-talk: "Even though a woman is negative to others, she'll never be negative to me," then later, "Well, I guess I'm better off than some people," and still later, "where is this going?" Along the way, he also added a few thoughts such as "Ignore it if a woman doesn't have her own life," and a few habits such as leaving extra-generous tips for waiters that his girlfriend had been rude to. (This is co-dependency.)

His coping behaviors were to enjoy the company of his many positive friendships, and to continue to tell himself to "forget about it, don't kick up a fuss, and accept that her behaviors and needs should trump mine."

Fortunately, by the time Jay came to see me, he was pretty tired of this cycle, and he was ready to set his intention to change whatever he had to change. One of the first things we had him do was read *Boundaries* by Anne Katherine, and he was able to recognize that while he had healthy boundaries in the other areas of his life, his boundaries around women were too weak because his internal relationship template was one of accommodation. He began to recognize that "giving in" all the time was how he signaled to a woman that his boundaries could be compromised. Jay understood that he would have to experiment with new thinking and quickly follow it up with new behaviors in order to send a different message. He also got it that his new thoughts and behaviors, even if they felt experimental, would help to break the energy pattern around him and would begin to attract a different outcome.

So, having broken up with girlfriend number four, he began by practicing the following new thoughts: "I should really look at the significance of a woman's negative behavior," "I want to choose an energizing partner who is healthy," "It is a bad sign if a woman gets drunk on a first date," "I can just be a friend before deciding whether to pursue a romantic relationship," and "I deserve a true fit."

He noticed that that made him feel a bit more empowered, but he knew that the feelings would have to be followed up with behavioral change, so he began limiting phone calls from his ex, then proceeded to block her numerous calls and text messages. He also set better boundaries with women he was dating, asking for clarity if he got mixed messages from them, and even cutting back on some dating relationships and some friendships if he sensed a woman had things to work on. He found he was better respected by the healthier women, and was able to ignore the pleadings and drama of the less healthy women.

In a short time, Jay felt positioned for the success he desired. He had set his intention to change, become aware of his unhealthy self-talk, determinedly developed new thinking, practiced new behaviors even if he couldn't yet see the outcome, and so he changed the energy field within himself and around him. In time he became aware that he had altered his relationship template. His openness to change habitual thoughts and behaviors had signalled to the Universe that it could realign itself to deliver what he was seeking. He felt different, "more on top of things than ever before," as he described it, more observant, more empowered. Jay had cleared the static out of the way so he could hear his Inner Voice guide his search for a mate. Mr. Nice Guy had gained control of his life.

When you're stuck, you absolutely have to start changing your thoughts, but sometimes your biochemistry can play a role in making it hard to practice new self-talk or to hear your Inner Voice. Darlene had this experience, but she overcame it quickly with the right support:

Overcoming Fear: Darlene's Story

At 28, Darlene was in the most stuck place in her life she had ever been. Coming out of a big family where she had felt "lost in the shuffle," she craved a sense of belonging and so married her high-school boyfriend at age 20. With little education and few work skills, she quickly had two kids, and found herself isolated in a marriage that was growing increasingly tense and unfulfilling. She struggled with depression, and over the course of a few years she was prescribed six different anti-depressants. None of them worked, and over time her despair led to feeling suicidal. One day, six years into the marriage, Darlene's husband announced he was leaving.

To her horror, Darlene found herself a single mother with a huge mortgage, a pile of debt, and a mountain of fear. She had lacked the resources and knowledge to secure an effective, enforceable separation agreement with appropriate financial support and child support, and so she quickly found herself in the position of having to sell her home to stay solvent. She then realized that unless she threw herself on the mercy of her family, she and her children would be homeless.

Fortunately, a brother who lived on the other side of the country came to the rescue, offering her and her kids a place to stay while she got re-established. Darlene knew it would mean leaving all her other supports, but lacking any alternative she packed up her kids and a few belongings and made the lonely journey across the country, heading into an uncertain future.

In a short time, depression and fear took over. Living in an expensive city, she lacked the kind of credentials that would allow her to secure an adequately-paying job or affordable housing.

She had no friends in her new city, and she couldn't see a future for herself and her children. That is when she came to see me.

As you can probably guess by now, Darlene had healing to do in all four Domains. She had a unique biochemistry that left her vulnerable to stubborn depression. She also carried considerable sadness from her experience growing up in her family and so her History and her Brain and Body together reinforced her depression. She had lots of experience that had reinforced pessimistic beliefs about life, and so her self-talk was full of defeat and hopelessness. And to top it off, when I asked her about her spiritual resources, she said she was a "recovering Catholic, full of guilt."

I knew we would have to heal her History to clean out the roots of her depression, but I also saw that she wasn't strong enough to do that without having her depression alleviated somewhat first. So in spite of her unsuccessful track record with medication, I encouraged her to talk to her doctor about one of the latest-generation antidepressants that act on serotonin. We began gentle healing processes while we waited a few weeks for the anti-depressant to kick in, and then we ramped up, determinedly cleaning out her History with EMDR. She responded well.

We scheduled her a free consultation with a community lawyer so she could begin to address her child support issues. We pored through on-line information about housing, education and financial support, finding programs for her to follow up. And then we went to work on her self-talk.

Darlene's "garbage tape" that played automatically in her head went something like this: "I'm a failure, I can't get it together, I always get dead-ended somehow, I'm stuck." I helped her look at how the tape played loudly sometimes, and other times — more insidiously — outside of her awareness. When I asked her what body cues accompanied that tape, she realized her body felt listless, heavy and that she felt tearful. So what were the resulting feelings? Sadness, resignation, hopelessness, despair, and indecision.

And then, of course, we looked at the behaviors she was using to self-soothe or escape. Eating or over-eating was a favorite, resulting in a troublesome weight gain. Self-isolating and procrastinating were two others. And so, Darlene could see, the problem was still there. Not only did her behaviors not solve any part of the problem, but the outcome of them reinforced her beliefs that she would fail, be dead-ended and remain stuck.

I told Darlene about her relationship to the quantum energy field around her, and I explained how her thoughts were producing energy not only within her, but also an energy that emanated from her out into the world around her. I explained to her how her unchecked and unmanaged thoughts were sending out instructions to the quantum field, and how the field was aligning itself with her beliefs and delivering more of the same. I explained to her what a powerful person she really is, but that she had to use the power consciously or it will produce deadly feedback. She "got" it.

Darlene began to deliberately think grateful thoughts: for the shelter and support provided by her brother, for her beautiful kids, for the free legal consultation, for the right anti-depressant and for *potential* blessings that might come out of the education, housing and financial programs she was investigating. She noticed that when she *chose* to think these kinds of thoughts she felt better.

Then she decided she was ready to do the next step: practice new behaviors. So she started to do a little meditation/intention process (more on that in the next chapter), focusing on successes she wanted her kids to have at school. When she quickly got results, her surprise and delight motivated her to continue to express gratitude, and also to do some visioning/intention for her own life. Almost immediately, she found her ideal job-training program on-line. The health care system, in need of qualified medical assistants, was offering a one year training program that led to guaranteed employment at a good wage. She applied and was accepted. She was ecstatic!

And of course, her beliefs were changing. She had discovered that allowing her old beliefs to operate unchecked in her brain was keeping her stuck. So now when she recognized negative thinking going on, she shut it off as quickly as she could and formulated thoughts of gratitude for what she currently had, and for what she *would* have. She did this *even if she didn't feel like it.* She followed up these thoughts with behaviors that would open the door for change to enter, *even if she didn't feel like it.* She made herself take steps even when she would have preferred to self-isolate, avoid or procrastinate. She decided to engage a really competent lawyer to go after her ex-husband, to obtain the financial support her children deserved. She did the homework the lawyer asked her to do, locating and organizing all the documents her lawyer needed to proceed, and so the legal process (of which she had been so afraid) was set in motion.

She started to develop feelings of hope, of competence, and she began to see a future for herself and her children. She was no longer ruled by fear.

Darlene had learned that it was her *thoughts* that had been keeping her fear alive. She became determined to use her thoughts differently, and each time she did, she dispelled fear. She learned that her *intention* sent a powerful ripple effect out into the universe to create the kinds of outcomes she desired. This began to cause her to think differently about the religious training she had received. She realized that the God she had learned about was there for her, but that the relationship worked better when she used the co-creating powers she'd been given. How surprising to discover that life worked better when, rather than asking and hoping, she instead *intended and affirmed* that she was part of the divine molecular universe and therefore an inevitable recipient of its abundance. She could appreciate and enjoy God without the guilt.

Darlene looked forward to deliberately maintaining her positive inner dialogue, and to practicing success behaviors regardless of whatever negative feelings might be in the way on any given day. She saw that she could deliberately use her self-talk and new behaviors to *instruct* the universe about her intention to have a good job and to have child support. And she discovered that the feedback she received helped her hear her own Inner Voice saying "yes" to a new career path and to a legal plan of action. She "got it" that she was the architect of her success, and that she could use her power to continue to attract to herself greater and greater happiness. Darlene was well on her way to the life of her dreams.

You might be wondering by now what Julie Jones' self-talk sounded like. When we last left her in Chapter Two, she had done some healing on her history, but had stopped before it was complete, moving away with a man. Her self-talk hadn't become healthy enough yet, and so she couldn't hear her Inner Voice accurately. Her relationship template was still distorted, and so she could only attract someone who devalued her. When things went sour, she came back to town, ready to resume her healing.

When we tuned in to her self-talk, here's what gradually unfolded:

Julie Hears Her Inner Voice

Julie knew that she attracted adversity because of her unhealed past, but she hadn't yet learned to tune in to her inner narrative to hear how it was scripting her life. So when she came back to see me after her experiment with another relationship, as quickly as possible we zeroed in on that inner script, and this is what we heard: "I make a lot of bad decisions, there are a lot of not-good people, I can't trust myself, there's something wrong with me, I'm not going to let someone bully me, and I'm tired of people not being accountable." Can you hear how she went from self-blame, to fear, to self-criticism, all of which is tiring and leads nowhere, and so from there to defensiveness and anger?

What were also underlying those thoughts were some even deeper ones like: "I'll never be loved, I have to put up with bad treatment in order to have a relationship, it's just the way it is..."

Julie recognized, too, that her feelings always recycled through frustration, hopelessness, despair, anger, and ultimately ended in *loneliness*. And no wonder, since her inner dialogue alternated between two poles, both of which led to the same end: either everything was her fault, and therefore she'd never be worthy to attract love, or it was someone else's fault, and her anger would turn people off and keep her alone.

To discharge her feelings, she had often spent time checking out on-line dating sites or with friends at the bar, looking for guys. And it had led to some difficult dating experiences, and ultimately nowhere.

Julie's self-talk was deeply entrenched. Her pattern of feeling lonely, then setting herself up for more loneliness was likewise well-anchored. Her lack of meaningful places to belong perpetuated her pain, given that she had no real connection to family, was single and had no other community, cultural or spiritual affiliations. It was clear that Julie needed some brand new information to introduce into her inner dialogue, and that that information might be most helpful if it gave her a larger context of meaning in which to view her life. So one day I gave Julie information about the quantum universe, and about her molecular/energetic relationship to it. I got her to take a look at how her old beliefs and thoughts continued to send out "instructions" to the universe, and how as a powerful person she could use her thought processes differently to produce different outcomes. Julie and I practiced a simple meditation/intention/visioning process in our session (details on this in the next chapter) and she agreed to practice it briefly, but daily, at home.

She "got it" that she had to stay aware of her negative self-talk in order to interrupt the "instructions" she had been sending out, and that she had to daily affirm her powerful relationship to the universe. She also got it that practicing gratitude thoughts would be essential, *whether she felt like it or not.* She understood that as soon as you shut off old negative thinking, you have to fill that air space very quickly.

She began to experiment with thoughts like: "I'm on a learning curve — I'm learning to listen to my Higher Self/The Universe and be guided to better and better decisions; there are lots of good people and I choose to focus on them now; I can trust myself now — I've learned the lesson, I have the knowledge; I'm perfect in my imperfection; I draw respectful people into my life and it's demonstrated in their behaviors; I don't have to be the one to correct this person in their journey."

Julie began to get absolutely stunning results with the daily meditation/intention/visioning process because it forced her to shut off her negative self-talk and fill the air space with healthier instructions for the universe to respond to. She started to feel more optimistic, and more willing to practice new behaviors. She started to hear her Inner Voice telling her that she could have very different outcomes, that she deserved happiness after all. In the next chapter, I'll tell you about Julie's stunning results.

By now you can probably see how important it is to make sure your Brain and Body are healthy, that the troubling aspects of your History are healed, and that you remain conscious at all times of how your Self-Talk is operating. If you have attended faithfully to the first three Domains of Healing, you should be feeling pretty good. You should be noticing that dysfunctional old patterns have faded away, and that you are beginning to hear your authentic Inner Voice. This Inner Voice may be quiet or loud, and it may express itself gradually or sometimes all at once. You may begin to hear its message about whether the relationships you're in are good for you, about whether the job or school program you are pursuing is aligned with your deepest talents and highest good, about whether it is time to pursue some delayed dreams or take some healthy risks. And because you have some healing under your belt, and tools to shut off negative self talk, you can begin to hear a deep sense of truth within you about many aspects of your life. With the first Three Domains in good working order, you should begin to feel in charge of your life and optimistic about your future. You have built a strong foundation for your self-transformation — not unlike that of the Great Pyramid: solid, balanced, able to withstand the elements and reflecting the beauty within and without.

But if you are not feeling as balanced, solid, strong and happy as you should, if you want additional tools to support you in your journey, or if you want to ramp up to even higher levels of happiness, The Fourth Domain, Your Connection to the Universe, is awaiting you. It is your portal into the Field of All Possibilities. The things you will learn to do in the Fourth Domain are exciting beyond your imaginings.

Let's take a look…

Chapter Four

AM I ALL ALONE IN THIS?

The Fourth Domain of Healing:
Your Connection to the Universe

"Music in the soul can be heard by the Universe."
Lao Tzu, philosopher of ancient China

"Follow your bliss and the Universe will open doors … "
Joseph Campbell, mythologist, writer, lecturer

WHAT IS THE point of healing your Brain and Body, your History and your Self-talk? So that you can live big! So that **nothing** stands in the way of your access to the quantum field. As you know by now, your Body, your pool of experience and observation, and the way you talk to yourself can be limiters of your World View, and they can either link you to the Field of All Possibilities or keep you from it. But with healing underway in the first Three Domains, you are ready to drastically expand the boundaries around you and to open channels to produce outcomes beyond your experience, and beyond your past imaginings.

The Field of All Possibilities

Let me first expand a little on what I've told you about the quantum universe, the Zero Point Field. Quantum thinking is that the universe or Zero Point Field, or the Field as it is called, is the pool of all energy. It is all around you. And since everything that has ever happened, is happening or will happen is an energy transaction, quantum thinking suggests that past, present and future are all enfolded in the Field.

Let me say that again: past, present and future are not arranged on some linear continuum in the sky. In fact, past, present and future are simply ideas or constructs that we use on this planet to make sense of our experience. Time itself does not exist — it is a system of measurement that we use on this planet to make sense of things. Einstein said that Time is relative to where you are positioned when you observe something, which means that "time" can speed up or slow down. (If you have ever watched Stanley Kubrick's movie "2001: A Space Odyssey" you will have an idea of how moving at the speed of light can make it seem as though time is barely passing.) Quantum physics tells us that what we think of as Past, Present and Future are in fact all just energy vibrating together in the quantum field. All the events and material things of Past, Present and Future are simply energy temporarily slowed down into something visible. But when that energy is finished being in that form, that thing, or that event, it simply returns to the quantum field. All that has ever existed or will exist is contained or dispersed in the quantum field.

The most exciting thing about this is that because all things that have yet to happen or materialize do exist in the quantum field, all possibility and probability exist in the quantum field, all around you! This means you are connected to, and part of, the Field of All Possibilities. Research shows that because gentle intention by human beings can affect the behavior of other molecular matter and energy fields, *your gentle intention can affect the quantum field, affect future outcomes, and materialize desired possibilities. This means that when you use your energy through intention, you reach into the quantum field and affect what probabilities will split off and show up in your life. You direct the quantum field to translate a possibility into an actuality in your very own life!*

It's like the River of All Possibilities runs through your living room — it's that close. You can reach into it by using directed thought (intention) and pulling towards you whatever you focus on. Or it's like using your thoughts to reach through an invisible curtain, gently take hold of an event, thing or outcome you desire, and pull it back through the curtain into this dimension! (And as you will see in a minute, there are a few steps to accompany this process which help to ensure it really produces your dreams.)

As "new age" as all this sounds, it's actually knowledge that has been around for millennia. Throughout the ages, sacred traditions all over the world have taught their followers that we are visible beings in the midst of a vast invisible sea of creative energy. And these same traditions have taught that thought shapes outcome. Most of these traditions have passed down specific knowledge about how to direct thought in the form of prayer, meditation, mindfulness or consciousness to create outcome. It's only lately that science has caught up with this knowledge.

In fact, it is because directed thought and intention are so powerful, that throughout modern history — particularly since the time of Christ — various political empires have sanctioned or informally relied upon some churches and religious bodies to insert themselves as intermediaries between humans and the metaphysical world. This served to separate people from very real power and to make them more easily subservient to a political regime. Individuals were gradually robbed of their inherent connection to the metaphysical universe, to the divine, and were trained to believe that accessing those larger forces could occur *only* through a designated "holy person." Layers of fear became added into spirituality, and distortions grew, particularly the notion that inherent "sinfulness" required one to work towards worthiness, and to receive absolution from an intermediary holy person. Thus grew the phenomenon of "dualism," the concept that we are separate from the divine or the Field, that It is not part of us, that we are not part of It, and/or that if we are connected, the effectiveness of the connection is conditional on an intermediary, or on "worthiness." (Fortunately, in modern times many healthy churches and religious organizations have overcome this heritage, and are themselves a powerful positive link to the divine for their members.)

You can see that quantum physics supports ancient spiritual wisdom, and suggests that the physics of the Universe not only connect you to all that is, but are in fact set up to serve you in exercising very real power. Quantum physics show us that it is *not* a dualistic universe, and you don't need an intermediary to make powerful things happen. No longer do we need to "hope," "try to have faith," "hope that we are worthy," or fear that a great moral Judge might find us wanting and "punish" us by saying "no."

The physics are set up so that you are *already* connected to the end-lessly generative Universe. That's right — endlessly generative. The

Universe can't help itself. It is the Great Recycler of all energy, and it is always looking for a way to express. It will push up weeds through cracks in the sidewalk, grow alpine flowers on nothing but a patch of rock, turn ashes (gradually) into rose bushes, and constantly replace the dead with the living. It is so endlessly growth-producing that it will multiply cancer cells if it is given the right conditions to do so. And while the Universe may appear to produce random growth, it actually responds to our directions. It will generate specific forms of matter when we give it instructions or a recipe to do so — that is what reforestation programs are based on, what vineyards depend on, what parents hope for on when they conceive and pass on their genetic gifts to their developing offspring.

Accessing the Field of All Possibilities

So how wisely are you giving instructions to the endlessly generative Field? By this point it's probably pretty clear that when you live unconsciously (i.e. when you don't pay attention to what you're thinking) you are sending out a mixture of signals to the quantum field. Some days you hope for or expect good things to happen, other days you cancel out those thoughts with pessimistic or angry thinking. The quantum field hears an intermittent set of instructions from you, or two completely contradictory sets of instructions, so it can't align itself with your heart's desire.

But as you take care of unhealed issues in the first Three Domains, as your Brain and Body, your History and your Self-Talk begin to get cleaned up, you are better positioned to send out instructions in a way that will manifest your dreams. And while simply thinking positively can help move you in the direction of your desires, there is a way to get much better results, to get fantastic results!

So how exactly do we access that great quantum field, that vibrating sea of creative energy? How exactly do we bring into being the tantalizing possibilities we've been dreaming about? Fortunately, people have been experimenting with these questions for so many centuries that there is now a pretty solid consensus about the six things that we must do to bring our dreams into reality. I've "road-tested" and refined my version of this knowledge, lived it with delightful results, taught it to my clients and witnessed their impressive results, and so I'd like to present to you:

The 6 Quantum Secrets to an Amazing Life!

1) Tune In to the Universe

What does that mean — "tune in to the Universe?" It can easily sound like a cliche. Do you get pictures of people sitting around cross-legged, chanting "ommm...?" Well, the fact is that chanting works beautifully for some people, and for others not at all! The important thing is: finding a comfortable, natural way to align yourself with the quantum field every day is the essential first step to manifesting your dreams.

Through the centuries, people have experimented with ways of getting on the same wave-length as the quantum field. They have found that it happens best when they quiet themselves, let go of distractions, slow down, and focus on a sense of what is beautiful, peaceful, powerful and loving about the Universe. There are as many ways to do this as there are people in the world. Buddhists, for example, focus on their breathing, empty themselves out, chant a mantra (a simple repetitive sound) and as they do so they gradually shift from an alert state characterized by "beta" brainwaves, to a relaxed state characterized by slower "alpha" or even deeper "theta" waves. Many people use the process of focusing quietly on a beautiful scene or object such as a flower or a stone, and immersing themselves in the beauty of that focal point. Some spiritual traditions use a favorite prayer as a way of shifting into an awareness of divine and loving energies in the quantum field. Some folks repeat a favorite prayer many times, and find that as they do so, the rhythm of the words shifts them into an "alpha" state, much like repeating a mantra does. Many people use visualizing processes such as picturing and feeling a white light or flow of energy flooding their being. These processes are often described as "meditative," and the practice of them as "meditation."

The age-old tradition of being still as the means of tuning in to the Universe merits some re-examination in modern times. While it is a wonderful ideal and practice, I treat a lot of people with modern attention problems such as ADD and ADHD, and for many of them, it is excruciating to have to sit still. Believing that they must be able to achieve stillness, many of these folks have turned away from traditional meditation practices, and they have shunned religious settings as well, feeling them to be too much like "school." They have assumed or even been told that because they don't "fit the mold" they cannot adequately achieve a connection with higher energies or with a sense of the divine.

What works well for many people is a more active way of tuning in to the generative, beautiful and healing energies of the quantum field. Lots of people use gentle dance, yoga and/or music to enter a relaxed focused state and tune in to the surrounding sea of higher energy in which we are embedded. For many, a favorite way of connecting to the power and abundance of the universe is to be walking in nature, surrounded by skies and open fields or mountains and valleys. And around the world, many people have found that shamanic and traditional native spiritual practices such as drumming help them shift from an alert beta state into the more receptive alpha or theta states.

Some people have had particularly troubling experiences with religious practices, and/or they have been exposed to meditation or spiritual practices that didn't feel right for them. For those folks, even seemingly-benign terms such as "Universe" or "higher energy" are off-putting. If that describes you, don't worry. One of the myriad ways this process can be done is to tune in to whatever you conceive of as your Higher Self.

And for the purely science-minded, just tune in to the wonder and complexity of the quantum field.

Whatever form of tuning in to the Universe you choose, use it as a time to be aware of a few important things:

- The quantum universe, whether you know it as God or as the Field, is the source of everything

- It is endlessly intelligent, abundant and generative

- You are part of it

- it is part of you

Picture or feel these things within yourself. Let your mind and being gently dwell on what they mean to you. When you do, you will align with the Universe, and with its energy and creativity. You will be in synchrony with its dynamic structure, with the dancing molecules and particles that can organize themselves to produce your dreams. Really! Don't worry if at first you can't feel or sense that you are aligned with the quantum field. In a very short time you will come to experience that this process really works. Just do it until you start to see the results — you won't be sorry! When I, and later many of my clients started this process, it was with a reserved wait-and-see attitude. That's fine. The Universe respects you for showing up, and so it will show up for *you*.

≈≈≈ Brain Waves ≈≈≈

Because certain states of awareness are known to lead to better connections with the quantum field, let me give you a little more information about the beta, alpha and theta states of your brain. Your brain will shift from one of these states to another as you tune in to the Universe, so you may as well know a bit about what's going on inside your head! For starters, the most alert of our brain waves are beta waves. Your brain is probably in beta as you are reading this. Beta waves can be low, medium or high, and are typically produced when we are focused on a task. If we are tense about the task, and feeling intense emotions such as anger or anxiety, beta waves are high. If we have a somewhat narrow focus but are not tense, we tend to produce medium beta waves. If we are interested and gently focused, but not tense, we tend to produce low beta waves. Of the three beta states, it is only in the relaxed low beta state that we can begin to tune in to the Universe.

Gradually we may shift into an alpha state, in which we are still alert, but our focus is softening and our muscles are further relaxing. This is an even more receptive state in which to connect to higher energies of the quantum field.

With more experience, we may find that we shift into deeper theta waves when we tune in to the Universe. Theta waves are also produced during "twilight consciousness," daydreaming, or falling asleep. Buddhist monks who have been studied during their meditation produce these deep waves. Research shows that while we can begin to tune in to the Universe in a low beta state, it is in a relaxed alpha state or the deeper theta state that we are the most likely to feel connected to the Universe. In alpha or theta we develop a sense of oneness with all things, and experience shifts in consciousness. In alpha and theta we are more likely to feel that we connect with higher wisdom, and even to experience the mystical.

And if you are new at tuning in to the Universe, or are overcoming attention deficit issues, there's good news: you can get into alpha without forcing yourself!! In fact, the lovely paradox is that you *can't* force alpha or theta. Rather, it is when you simply gently focus on whatever connects you to your sense of the infinite, let go, and don't try to "produce" an alpha state, that you are the most likely to spontaneously shift into alpha (or even theta, with more experience.) In fact, alpha is really a pretty natural state for us; it's just that the rush and hurry of modern life keeps a lot of people in beta, and has caused a lot of people to "forget" their natural skill at accessing, deepening and sustaining alpha.

Dr. Les Fehmi, director of the Princeton Biofeedback Centre in Princeton, New Jersey describes an easy way to shift into alpha. He discovered it by accident one day in his lab while working with research subjects. Having tried a number of peaceful ways to induce alpha, without success, he simply asked his subjects "can you imagine the space between your eyes?" Alpha appeared instantly on the brainwave monitors! And when he instead asked "can you imagine the space between your ears?" alpha again instantly appeared. Over time, Dr. Fehmi discovered that when he asked his subjects to imagine space between and around body regions, then through the body, then extending limitlessly in every direction, their brains dropped effortlessly into whole-brain synchronous alpha. He also discovered, to his amazement, that this relaxed state of awareness, and corresponding alpha brain waves, could be accomplished with eyes open.[17] So there are some pretty easy ways to ready yourself to connect to the higher energies of the quantum field!

Once people have the basic idea of how to tune in to the Universe, many people wonder if it matters where or when they tune in. Well, it works best if you do it every day. As you'll see, we're going to add in a few steps to get you manifesting your dreams, and in order to send out consistent instructions about those dreams to the Universe, you pretty much need to be doing it daily. But don't make it a "should," or your energy won't line up with what you're trying to accomplish. The Universe just needs to know that you are thinking of it, so it can be thinking of you. Just set aside about 15 minutes each day to relax and enjoy this process.

I find it works best if I do it in the morning, but I have had good results with doing it in the evening, too. One of my clients, a creative single mother who is often pressed for time, recently told me that she sometimes tunes in to the Universe only briefly in the morning, and tells It that she will set

---

17 Fehmi, L. and J. Robbins. 2007. *The Open-Focus Brain*. Boston: Trumpeter/ Shambhala.

aside more time in the evening to tune in, express gratitude and set her intentions. When she tunes in during the evening, particularly when she moves into the steps designed to send intention, she asks the Universe to send her intention backward in time to apply to the whole day! She really gets it that in the quantum field there is no past, present or future, and that intention can influence the Field from any point in "time," so she knows that as long as she is regular about it and does it with positive intention, she'll accomplish what she wants to. And she is manifesting all kinds of fun things, which tells her she is on the right track.

I've also found that on very busy days, I can tune into the Universe for shorter periods throughout the day wherever I am. Although I normally prefer to tune in at home in the morning in a quiet room, I'll also do it briefly at a stop-light in the car, sitting on the staircase at my lunch break, or even standing in the vestibule as I leave the office. These work well for me as a temporary alternative, although I most enjoy getting close to the loving and creative forces in the Universe when I set aside time in the morning in my preferred environment. But a relationship with the Universe is a lot like a relationship with a lover or partner — you might not always have a quantity of quality time together every day, but little bursts of quality interaction throughout the day (as you would with an e-mail, a text, or a note) can keep your connection strong. Tuning in to the Universe at a stop-light, at your office, or while washing the dishes can be a secret pleasure that keeps you aligned with quantum energies.

The most important thing is to just enjoy tuning in to the Universe. Just relax in the way that's best for you, and let yourself focus on your sense of the infinite sea of creative energy that is around you and within you. If you have a distractible "monkey brain," as some meditators call it, just notice it. Don't judge it. Higher energies will align with you as you gently bring your thoughts back to the creative, alive, infinite, abundant Universe.

And as you'll see next, in the process that I like to teach, you're going to get actively involved with the Universe shortly after you tune in to it, so getting distracted by other things tends not to be a problem.

2) Express Gratitude!

Gratitude greases the wheels of your connection to the quantum field. Centuries of spiritual and metaphysical practice have corroborated the truth of this. Gratitude puts you into a circuit with the quantum field. So as soon as you have tuned in to the Universe, begin to express your gratitude to it. Whether you think of it as a deity or as the Field, it contains the totality of all that is, and that's pretty awesome. Thank it for whatever focal point is helping you to connect — whether it's a mountain, a sunset, a beautiful baby, a religious artifact such as a cross, a spiritual object such as a feather or sweetgrass, the sound of the Tibetan bells you might be listening to, or the flow of Reiki energy through your being. I often just thank it for all the energy that has kindly slowed down to serve as molecules of matter in my life, whether it's my home or my friends for example. I'll often thank it for molecules of matter that have slowed down into energy transactions such as a thoughtful gesture from someone or the healing that one of my clients experiences. It puts us into a feedback loop with the universe to thank it for things large and small, past and recent, and for things to come. I like to review the good things that have happened in the previous 24 hours, and thank the energies of the quantum field for lining up to produce those good things. As I review those things, it strengthens my awareness of how truly responsive the Field is, and strengthens my certitude that the things I envision and intend today will just as surely show up.

As you'll see in a moment when we discuss how to set your intention for things, it is very important to thank the Universe ahead of time for the things you intend to manifest. Remember, all things already exist in the quantum sea of all possibilities, and you are simply using intention to bring chosen outcomes into the here and now. When you say thank you for that situation, event or thing ahead of time, you are sending instructions into the quantum field to start selecting out that probability from all the probabilities surrounding it. When you say thank you ahead of time, it is like giving your credit card information when you order something from a store. You wouldn't give your credit card information unless you were intending to receive the item, and it's the same with the

Universe — give it "credit" for what it is about to send your way.

Having said that, I want to affirm that I believe it is critical to express gratitude without having to have something in return. The Universe happens to be very generous and will endlessly direct bounty your way, especially once you learn this process. But you are in a relationship with the Universe, and just as in human relationships, the connection doesn't deepen if we only express gratitude when it's about something we asked for. Our gratitude needs to be expressed at all times with as much sincere feeling as possible. It is the *feeling* of appreciation that connects us with the Universe, not simply the words.

As you will see when we talk about "planting seeds" in a minute, it is our actions that affirm to the Universe that we are serious about what we intend. Similarly, grateful *behaviors* are as important as grateful words or feelings. So find ways of quietly expressing your gratitude in the world around you. Practice random acts of kindness — plug someone's parking meter, buy the person behind you a cup of coffee, let someone into traffic. This keeps you in a powerful loop with the quantum field, and your days will just get more abundant.

3) Set Intentions for Others. Affirm for Others.

Our ability to positively influence the quantum field depends upon our sense of the inter-connectedness of all things. Centuries of experience and decades of research tell us that. So when we set and focus positive intentions for others, we hook into that vast sea of interconnected energies. Our positive intentions for others create a powerful energy field linking us to the source of all abundance. The plans and intentions we have for our own lives unfold in the context of this interconnectedness; they don't happen in isolation.

So how do you go about setting intention for someone else? What is appropriate when you are focusing on someone else's life? Here are some guidelines:

- When you have a specific request from someone, or have a pretty good idea of what they might need, visualize and/or feel what it is they need. Picture or feel it *already accomplished.* Don't forget, the outcome already exists in the quantum field. It is your gentle intention, accompanied by visualizing and/or feeling the result that splits off that outcome from the pool of probabilities surrounding it and readies it to manifest in the here and now. So for example, if your cousin Jane is battling pneumonia, picture and feel her fully healthy, her pneumonia nowhere in sight. Picture and feel her enjoying that health in as much detail as you like. Send warm caring energy into the picture.

- Accompany your visual and/or feelings with affirmative words. The affirmative words confirm and clarify to the Universe what the outcome will look like. So for example, you might say "I gratefully affirm that Jane is absolutely healthy, her lungs are clear and pink, her breathing is easy and comfortable, and she is able to do everything with ease." Avoid using language that keeps the problem alive. For example, it's better *not* to say "I affirm that Jane doesn't have pneumonia, her coughing is gone, her fever is down." Let your language be about her as though she never had pneumonia.

- Go a bit further by stating why you know her health to be a given. For example, say "I gratefully acknowledge that all the molecules of the quantum field are happily lining up to accomplish this for Jane." Picture the molecules aligning themselves and sending health to Jane.

- Acknowledge the even larger reasons you know this to be true: "Health and peace and wellness in all forms are inherent in the quantum field. It is the nature of the quantum field to abundantly provide, and Jane is a member of the quantum field, so her health is a given. Also, that probability exists fully in the quantum field, so I simply invite it to be visible here."

- Should you be more specific? If it makes sense to do so, be as specific as possible: "I gratefully affirm that Jane is completely healthy now, and it is visible by her graduation day. She is able to easily partake in all the celebrations that day." Picture her at her graduation, smiling, healthy and energetic.

- What do you do when you're not clear what the perfect outcome should be? For example, maybe another issue is that Jane passionately wants to get into nursing school, but you just can't see her as a nurse. Go ahead and set your intention for her, but be general. Picture her smiling and happy in the future, but leave the setting vague. Send warm caring energy into the picture. Affirm that "Jane is accepted into the right program for her highest good, that she is guided to her true path, that she is happy in her education and career, and that all things unfold to make that possible." Affirm that the quantum field now aligns to arrange the ideal outcome for Jane. Send your gratitude into the quantum field for its generosity in arranging things for Jane.

- Whether you are setting a specific intention or a general intention for someone, repeat the above processes each day until the outcome is manifest. But don't forget, *gentle* intention is what moves the Universe, so while it doesn't hurt to repeat your intention several times each day, your repetition should be gentle, affirmative and grateful, not urgent or insistent.

- While you are awaiting an outcome, it is your gratitude that tells the Universe you consider it a *fait accompli* or a "done deal." Nothing says "mission accomplished" like gratitude. Gratitude is your part of the transaction. Gratitude affirms to *you*, not just to the Universe, that the outcome is accomplished. And don't worry if you can't always deeply feel the gratitude; while that is preferable if you can feel it, what's most important is that you make the effort to express the gratitude as sincerely as possible. The Universe knows that you are only human and sometimes can't fully feel the outcome. Your *behaviors* directed towards the desired outcome are a powerful magnet for the outcome to show up. And the quantum field is amazingly generous about actually increasing your feelings of certainty if you just keep at it. It will honor your effort.

- Each day when you do your intentions, try expressing gratitude for everything the quantum field did in the last 24 hours to move Jane towards health or towards her perfect career. (It doesn't matter that you can't yet see or know what the quantum field did about your intention.) Don't forget, we can direct intention backward in time to affect probabilities in the quantum field, so when you express gratitude for activities in the past 24 hours you are still influencing the field.

- Think about keeping a journal of your intentions for others, and record the outcomes as they manifest. This is a very powerful tool to affirm the workings of the quantum field. On days when you need a boost you can review your journal and remember not only all the good things the quantum field has delivered, but that it was your intentions that made them happen!

4) Set Intentions for Yourself. Affirm for Yourself.

Now you are ready to set intentions for your own life. You have tuned in to the Universe, expressed gratitude, and affirmed good things for others. This aligns and connects you with the highest energies, and puts you in a very powerful place to send out to the Universe the blueprint for your desired life. And don't worry if you can't feel all of those things. Just go ahead and do the process. The Universe will really honor you for doing it when you can't yet see or feel tangible results. And as you start to get results (you will!) it will make it easier and easier to do this process every day. In fact, you will likely feel quite drawn to your meditation/intention time because of what starts to happen.

This part of your process is very similar to the part in which you have affirmed for others. It operates with all the same principles, but there are a few additional elements. For example, when you are setting intentions and affirming them in your own life, it is particularly helpful to design short-term, medium-term and long-term outcomes, so that every day you have new successes, imminent successes on the horizon, and long-term successes that are still hovering unseen in the quantum field. Think of planting and harvesting a garden. When you tend a garden, it's really rewarding to have some plants that come up very early in the spring, while there is still snow on the ground. These early plants remind us of what is yet to come. And it is also really fun to have some annuals that grow only for one season — they provide variety and allow for experimentation. A wise gardener also plants biennials and perennials — plants that are worth waiting for, as they are hardy, beautiful and come up for years. If you are planting short, medium and long-term goals, you always have things to be grateful for, always have visible results in your life, and always have affirming evidence that additional long-term dreams are in process.

As well, it is helpful to have small, medium and large goals, because the Universe can often arrange a small goal to manifest quickly, while larger goals can sometimes take a bit more time to align and manifest. Just as in gardening, you always plant a balance of things — it is the contrast between small, medium and large that creates beautiful diversity in life.

It is also really helpful to break up your biggest goals into "sub-goals." For example, if you want to be a successful artist, each day you design, intend and affirm goals that move you towards that outcome. So you might affirm that "this week I attract to myself information about the best art schools or art studios in this city." You'll express gratitude ahead of time for that outcome and you'll plant seeds towards this goal by researching on-line or talking to people at art shows. As the week progresses, you might begin to design, intend and affirm that "over the next month I attract advice from successful artists, and information about where I can get the best, least expensive art supplies." You'll express gratitude ahead of time for that outcome, and gratitude every day as the quantum universe begins to arrange it. You'll plant seeds towards that outcome by putting yourself in places where you can find those art supplies and have those conversations. As the weeks and/or months progress, and you find yourself enjoying these outcomes, you'll set more and more goals related to your long-term goal: that someone asks you to paint a portrait for their child's birthday, that someone hears of your work and invites you to submit something to a local art show, that your work gets mentioned in the local newspaper. As you keep gently focused on your goals, and as you send out affirmative instructions to the Universe, it will fertilize your thinking. You'll find yourself dreaming up more ways for the Universe to express its support for your goals, and you'll hear yourself offering diverse pathways for the Universe to manifest your dreams. Before you know it, your dreams are reality, visible and manifest in your life.

As I've mentioned, the overall process of intending and affirming for your life is otherwise very similar to your intending and affirming for others. Below I'll list all the steps, and I think you'll find that seeing the similarities helps strengthen your understanding of the process:

- After tuning in and expressing gratitude, set your short-term and small intentions. For example, "I gratefully affirm that I find the perfect parking spot today at lunch-time when I have to do an errand downtown. It's exactly in front of the store, or as close to it as possible. Thank you Universe, for arranging it." Go ahead and picture the very spot you'd like, and send warm energy into the picture. Understand that the Universe will arrange it; it is a done deal. It exists in the quantum field. It is a probability, surrounded by lots of other probabilities. Your picturing of it and affirming it with positive feeling and words causes the other probabilities to collapse, shrink or dissipate. It is enough that you simply assume the outcome. Don't "ask," or start trying to "have faith," hope," or urgently "will" it to happen — those things get in the way. Just know it's on the way, the same way the sunrise tomorrow is on the way. Then leave it alone. If you wish, you can picture it on the way downtown, but only the same way you're going to picture the building you're driving towards: it's a given fact that it's there. As you pull into the spot, be grateful.

- Set your other small, immediate or short-term intentions. You can link these in with longer-term goals. For example, "today I gratefully affirm that my boss finds a short-term solution to the labor shortage in our department, and that I am able to leave the office on time. I also affirm that s/he begins to attract a long-term supply of staff for our department, and that going home on time is easily accomplished for all of us."

- Set your medium-size or medium-term intentions. For example, you've been affirming the short-term goal that you'll do well in your upcoming exams. Go ahead and link it into larger medium-term professional goals and even longer-term career objectives. In other words, see it linked to other successes that precede it and that follow it. For example, "I affirm that I study all the right things for my exams next week, and easily achieve the grades I need to qualify for my pilot's license. I affirm that these accomplishments pave the way to a great career in aviation." Know that it is a done deal. See yourself flying the plane. Send warm grateful energy into the picture. You simply offer your shopping list to the Universe, and it is happy to supply whatever is in your highest, best interests.

- Sometimes you won't know what is in your highest, best interests. You might have a passionate desire to be an architect, and if you are cultivating your relationship with the Universe, it will only guide you to your highest and best outcome. So you might not get into architecture school. You might be disappointed, and think "well, this intention process is not working." But hang in! If you stay in process with the quantum field, it always attracts to you events and outcomes that are in perfect alignment with your deepest self. Be grateful for *whatever* you attract, and wait to see some signposts along the way as to why you didn't get into architecture school. Very surprising things happen when you stay flexible in this way. For example, you end up going into Interior Design, because it was your backup plan, and that is where you meet your soul mate! If you'd gone into Architecture, you might have missed each other. Nothing happens by accident. Later you decide you still want to go into Architecture, and it turns out that because you have your Interior Design degree, you get credit for so many courses that you are able to do the program a full year faster! The important thing is to set your intention, gently hold it in consciousness, stay flexible and grateful, and work with what the quantum field brings you. If you have an intention that is off-base in some way, but are consistent about gratefully connecting with the Universe each day, you will always get corrective feedback.

- For the above reasons, when you are setting any intentions, whether small or large, near or far, use language that allows the Universe to deliver something even better than you could have imagined. For example, if you want to get into college in the fall, study hard, send out college applications to several colleges, and each day say "I gratefully affirm that I get accepted into my local college or an even better college if that suits my needs better." This allows the Universe flexibility to deliver the best option for you. There might be a reason that you should be at your local college to start, or there might be a reason, unknown to you, that Harvard is not the most suitable place for your particular dreams to materialize. If you are super-keen to get into Harvard, then affirm that the Universe handles the *timing* of this dream: "I affirm that I am accepted into the perfect college this fall, and that my life-long dream of going to Harvard materializes now or at a better time in my future."

- Set your long-term intentions in a manner similar to the above. And if you don't know what your long-term intentions are, go ahead and be general in your meditation. Say "I gratefully affirm that I now attract to myself all the ideas, conversations, synchronicities, and events that point me in the direction of my long-term happiness. I affirm that my happy future is already a done deal — it exists in the quantum field and I can't wait to see it! I affirm that as the days and weeks and months go by, clearer and clearer ideas come to me about how I should pursue my highest good." Then picture yourself, smiling and happy in your future, and send warm and grateful energy into that picture. As you wait for direction from the quantum field, stay observant. I like to say that the Universe sprinkles a trail of breadcrumbs through the forest, to show you the way. One little thing might not look like a trail, but shortly after it comes another little thing, then another, and if you are observant you begin to see that they are all pointing in the same direction.

• Or, let's say you have a specific thing that you need to decide about, but you feel ambivalent or confused about what to do, such as whether to have children for example. Use your intention process to say "I affirm that I now attract clarity about whether I should become a parent. Over the weeks and months ahead, I attract the circumstances and feedback that help me know what I need to know to make this decision. Many probabilities and possibilities exist for me in the quantum field, and I now gratefully attract the ideal answer, the perfect outcome for me." Then picture yourself content in your future, without details, and send warm appreciation into the picture. Do this every day, and don't be surprised when people start initiating conversations with you about parenting, or the person in the seat next to you on the plane is reading a really great book about parenting, or you happen to turn on the television to a special about fertility options for people who are trying to conceive later than is optimal, etc. You'll get the helpful information you need.

• You can see how you might want to really spend some time doing your intentions, if you want lots to happen today, tomorrow and in the future. If you don't have time to do all the stages of intention in the morning, break it up into smaller parts: immediate and short-term intentions in the morning, and longer-term intentions later in the day. And don't forget to do your intentions for others — they are part of how you stay linked to the inter-connected energies of the quantum field. I often do intentions for my clients in the morning, along with immediate and short-term intentions for my own life. Later in the day, at my leisure, I can immerse myself in designing, intending and affirming intentions for all the other aspects of my life. You might even do some of your long-term intentions on the weekend, when you can really spend time tuning in to the quantum field and envisioning your biggest dreams.

- Always express gratitude for exactly what you have right now. Your gratitude doesn't keep you attached to your unemployment, or your reduced work hours or your low bank account. What it does do is keep your energy very clean, and allows the Universe to *use* those conditions as a bridge to something better. I recommend language such as "I am grateful for whatever I will learn out of my unemployment (or reduced work hours or low bank account.) I affirm that I will only have these conditions as long as I need them, and that they are replaced by abundance." I have done this often, and it is amazing how quickly the Universe replaces something I don't like with something I do like.

- Be patient! It is actually easy to be patient about longer-term intentions if you are daily keeping track and being grateful for the smaller outcomes that keep accumulating. You will quickly come to feel that you are "in process" at all times, and so current impediments start to feel like part of your path to success. (After all, every sales person gets a certain number of "no's" in between the "yes's".) As well, unseen results start to feel as certain as the visible ones. You will start to find yourself anticipating with curiosity what happens next.

5) Plant the Seeds of Change

Your behaviors are the outward expression of your intention. Your behaviors are how you tell the Universe you're serious. Anyone can wish and hope for things, but what makes you actually manifest outcomes is your willingness to roll up your sleeves and put a little elbow grease into it. You see, when you are willing to engage in activities directed at the desired outcome, your behavior acts like a magnet, aligning molecular forces to attract the outcome towards you. And what is very cool is that you don't necessarily have to know where exactly to plant the seeds! You don't know exactly how the Universe is going to deliver a dream; all you have to do is keep your behaviors in alignment with your goals and affirmations. So if you intend to get a great job, you are going to put together a good resume, go to job fairs, be willing to go on interviews even if they're not for the "perfect" job, and treat your 9 to 5 job hunting day as though it is your job! The Universe will see that you are serious, and so your visualizing, your affirmations, and your behaviors will attract great results.

One of my clients, Brad, learned how to give the Universe multiple paths for expression. He had been puzzled about why he wasn't attracting a great job. He seriously wanted to work, but had been waiting for interviews for the perfect job. When he understood that this was limiting the ways the Universe could deliver, things began to change. He began to get it that by going on interviews at places that might not be perfect, he was opening himself up to illuminating conversations, synchronous meetings and well-connected people, all of which may be how he would get directed to his perfect job. His willingness to plant seeds by going on seemingly less-than-ideal interviews would give him valuable experience, and would make him really knowledgeable about the competition in his area of expertise! He got it that those kinds of experiences would bear fruit if he engaged in them as a way to show the Universe he was serious.

When we say to the Universe, "okay, I'm going to demonstrate that I am intent upon finding a great job/apartment/car/whatever, I don't have to know ahead of time where, I'm just going to assume that my actions will align the molecular universe to support me…" our energy is never wasted. And usually, we don't have to plant these kinds of seeds for too long, because our willingness sends a powerful energetic wave into the quantum field, and it vibrates back to us at an even higher frequency, bringing with it options and opportunities.

In the meantime, go ahead and visualize your perfect job. You may plant seeds in one place, and the job comes up in another — that's because *all things are interconnected.* It is your behaviors and efforts (the outward expression of your intention) that link seemingly insignificant events over here with spectacular outcomes over there.

Simply put, just go ahead and "act as if…" Act as if it is already accomplished, because it is. Act as if you can see the outcome, because you will shortly.

Or a more familiar way of thinking about it is to "fake it til you make it." You're not really faking anything; you're simply acting in accordance with what you know to be true. Since it's already accomplished in the quantum realm, your behaviors aligned toward your goal are perfectly congruent with reality.

Let me give you another example of planting seeds. My client Sheila was determined to buy her first house, but it was a very expensive housing market, and Sheila had a limited amount of money. She knew what areas of the city appealed to her, what square footage she wanted, and that she required a fireplace, lots of sunlight and hardwood floors. But it didn't look as if all her conditions could be met within her budget and in her preferred areas of town. Not to worry. Sheila got it that planting seeds would make things happen, so in addition to visualizing, affirming and being grateful for her imminent home, she diligently looked at all kinds of houses, including ones that seemed to be unlikely. She wanted new, but she looked at old too. She wanted fresh, but she looked at fixer-uppers as well. She kept providing the Universe with multiple avenues through which it could express. She held onto her vision while she did so, and kept thanking the Universe for whatever it was up to. And sure enough, one day her agent took her to a listing in one of her preferred areas. It was a townhouse that couldn't even be seen from the street, so hidden that she could have driven by it and not known. Through the door she stepped, onto hardwood floors, sunlight streaming in, facing her fireplace. Everything was brand new. It was priced exactly within her budget. As I write this, she just took possession, and is getting ready to move in!

Look for as many reasonable ways to plant seeds toward your desired outcome as you possibly can. And if you can't think of many, or any, make this part of your intention process! Affirm that you are attracting brilliant ideas about ways to plant seeds to grow your dream. And be sure to express gratitude ahead of time for those ideas. I have done this frequently, and it simply amazes me the ideas that occur to me effortlessly after I do so. The ideas sometimes come gradually, and if I follow them up right away, more ideas occur. This is the Universe working with you, and it always feels surprising to have these ideas sprout in what previously felt like barren ground.

6) Affirm that your Intentions are Accomplished.

This step is important beyond words. It is not some "p.s." that we attach to the process; rather it is the step that seals the deal, that confirms your powerful co-creating role with the Universe. Since ancient spiritual traditions have been a source of great wisdom about the process of manifesting, it is helpful to refer to how various spiritual traditions accomplish this step. In the Jewish, Christian and Muslim traditions, people say "amen" at the end of prayer. "Amen" means "so be it" or "let it be," and it is said in order to affirm the outcome of the prayer. In the much more recent New Thought movement, which began in the late 19th century and which is today a vibrant and diverse collection of spiritual thinkers and practitioners, the affirmation "and so it is" is used at the end of affirmative prayer and spiritual treatments.

The use of the phrase "amen" or "and so it is" affirms your intention. It says aloud to the quantum field that you are concluding your respectful invitation for it to begin to align itself with your envisioned outcome (or better!) The affirmative words you use at the end of your Six Step meditation/intention process send out a wave into the quantum field. These affirmative words hone in on a desired outcome that sits in the sea of probabilities, and cause that outcome to begin to split off from other probabilities. Your affirmative words send a vibrational frequency that calls your outcome to you.

Don't forget, the River of all Possibilities runs through your living room. It is wherever you are. It is not far; it is indescribably close. That means that the very outcome you desire is within easy reach. It is swimming in the river or sea of possibility, and you are standing right in that river or sea. Another way of saying this is that your desired outcome is hanging like ripe fruit, low on the branches, right beside you. That's why yearning, pining, urgency, insistence or doubt are out of place. Your visualization, your gratitude, your affirmative words are the forces that mobilize the quantum field to produce.

So as often as you desire, picture your chosen outcome, send warm appreciative energy into it, and use whatever affirmative words you wish:

"I now affirm that my outcome is accomplished,"

"I am grateful for the wonderful (whatever) that is moving from the quantum field into visibility here and now."

"I enjoy my health, my reliable vehicle, my exam success, my satisfying job, my ideal mate, my safe and exciting trip, my…"

And so it is…

A SUMMARY OF
THE 6 QUANTUM SECRETS TO AN AMAZING LIFE !

1. *Tune In to the Universe*

2. *Express Gratitude!*

3. *Set Intentions for Others. Affirm for Others.*

4. *Set Intentions for Yourself. Affirm for Yourself.*

5. *Plant the Seeds of Change.*

6. *Affirm that your Intentions are Accomplished.*

Special Strategies to Use with the Six Quantum Secrets

Your Six Quantum Secrets can be used throughout your journey. Together, they can accelerate your healing in the first Three Domains — Brain and Body, History, and Self-talk. They can be used when formal healing processes are finished. And in an ongoing way, throughout your life, they can incorporate special strategies to meet particular challenges in your life. You can adapt the Quantum Secret Process to address a unique problem, heal a left-over old wound, strengthen and mature your character, and combine it with other spiritual practices to strengthen outcomes. Your Quantum Secret Process can assist in a struggle with anger or resentment, or help overcome intrusive negative self-talk such as doubt. It can also be used to guide you in your darkest hour. Here are some creative suggestions for how to use your Six Quantum Secrets to ramp up to the highest levels of living:

Special Strategy 1: Sending Intention Back to the Origins of a Problem

Because past, present and future are co-mingled in the quantum field, and you are a member of the quantum field, quantum researchers believe that you have the unique ability to direct your thoughts back through time to original events. American psychologist and metaphysical researcher Dr. William Braud suggests that "seed moments" exist in the quantum field, and speculates that we can direct intention back to these moments which precede a chain of events. Lynne McTaggart, in her thought-provoking book *The Field,* extrapolates this idea to situations such as sending intention back in time to the origins of a disease. She proposes that we could influence the eventual outcome of a disease that is already in progress.[18]

The idea to keep in mind is that the events you are currently living through are not finished, that their ultimate outcome can be influenced from a number of places in "time." So for example, if you got fired from your job, you can and should use your daily intention process to affirm

---

18 McTaggart, L. 2002. *The Field*, p. 175

that you learn from the experience and that you find your ideal job. But in addition, you can direct intention back in time to the all the moments surrounding the event of being fired. You're not likely to reverse the fact that you were fired, but you can surround those events with a healing energy so that the probabilities that play out *now* are of a higher order than they would otherwise be. You can send your intention back so that the shocked angry you is quickly filled with peace and curiosity about the future. You can visualize yourself leaving your employer's office with relief or even excitement. You can affirm that "this event is a turning point in my life; I have attracted it because I am on the road to even greater things. I now gratefully affirm that this moment becomes the bridge to my highest good."

And of course, you can send intention back in time on behalf of someone else. Use the same principles: that you are not necessarily trying to reverse an event, only its ultimate outcome. Your gentle intention can surround the event with positive energy, influencing the ensuing effects of the event. This avoids getting into a struggle with the event itself. Your intention can be directed to affirm that the event (however dire) unleashes a series of positive outcomes for the person who is the object of your intention. I used this process to intend a positive outcome for a client who had survived being hit by a freight train. What then transpired was that her insurance coverage turned out to be enough to heal not only that incident, but also two earlier traumas. When she left my office after her last appointment, she said, "I can't believe it, but I'm actually grateful that I got hit by a freight train! If I hadn't, I never would have healed these other bad things!" So always err on the side of assuming that you can retroactively turn a negative event into a positive one. Your power to do so is not limited by the passage of time.

Special Strategy 2: Healing Old Wounds.

There is a special way of using the above strategy to direct intention backwards in time to help yourself heal. You can retroactively send reparative energy to a younger self, and direct your intention to bring your healed younger self forward in time into the present. Sheila, whose search for the perfect home I mentioned earlier, is a great example of this process:

Sheila Heals an Old Wound

Sheila is a clever, resourceful I.T. professional in her early 40s. Single, and temporarily living with her mom, she originally came to see me to help her heal a long-standing self-loathing. Her radar for healthy relationships had been impaired in the dysfunctional family in which she grew up, and so a recent betrayal by a man had left her with a sexually transmitted disease. Her self-loathing was deepened by this experience, and surrounded by the bleak energy of her unhappy family, she felt suicidal. We used a combination of EMDR and cognitive behavioral therapy to help her heal, and she felt more empowered over many of the effects of her family history and her STD. Then I taught her the Six Quantum Secrets process, and she absorbed it like a sponge! She became powerfully aware of her connection to the quantum field, and able to use her intention to manifest great outcomes like her new townhouse. We were not quite finished EMDR, however, and so not surprisingly, during this period Sheila noticed that she was still troubled by an underlying self-hatred that fed into a dislike of her body and an avoidance of men.

Although she was able to work around it much of the time, she had a belief that she would always feel this way. Her belief kept that wounded energy attached to her (past and present.) I knew that EMDR would help to dissolve these feelings, but Sheila had to take a break from therapy for a couple of months, and so we would not be able to finish her healing for a while.

So I told Sheila that in the meantime, when she does her daily intentions and affirmations using the Six Step process, she could direct healing energy back in time to her child self, where the original self-hatred got started. I invited her to consider that her child self exists in the quantum field, and that the wounds of her child self are simply a collection of energy. She could dispatch love into the quantum field directly to her child self, and send healing to bombard the slowed-down wounded energy that was attached to her child self.

She could use this process to dissipate the energy of the wound, to break it up and disperse it back into the quantum field. The idea immediately made sense to her, because she had been sending other intentions into the quantum field and manifesting cool things like her townhouse, hard-to-get concert tickets, a high-priced designer purse for next-to-nothing, and a renewal of her contract when many of her co-workers were being laid off.

So Sheila began a regular process of sending loving energy back to "little Sheila," understanding that she was re-writing history! She got it that she could encase little Sheila in a bubble of loving energy and shield her as she moved forward through time to join adult Sheila in the present, where adult Sheila would be able to take care of her. She got it that the actual events of her childhood and family were a collection of energies that she could choose to keep alive through her old beliefs, or that she could disperse those realities back into the quantum field and liberate herself. She got it that her directed intention could protect little Sheila and bring her intact into a different present and future.

Sheila also understood that statements such as "my issue is self-hatred" kept that reality alive, and gave it new life. She understood that to continue to refer to the man who gave her an STD as "my offender" kept her frozen in time as his victim. She saw the wisdom instead in referring to him as her "catalyst," because that brought a dynamic energy to the events that had resulted in the STD, and allowed that event instead to become a turning-point in her life.

Sheila also saw that her fierce efforts to put closure on her STD only kept it alive emotionally. She saw that by moving into a looser, more open-ended position she left lots of room for healing energy to work in her body. She saw that her gentle intention to be well would affect the quantum field more effectively.

But most of all, she saw that sending loving energy back through time to the seed moments in her childhood created a different "her" now. Her intention aligned the quantum field to make that so.

Special Strategy 3: Overcoming Resentments

What do you do if you suspect that resentment is in the way? Thoughts and feelings such as resentments, grudges, keeping score, judgments, envy, jealousy and prejudices are powerful impediments to manifesting positive outcomes. It doesn't matter if the resentment or the feelings are connected in some way to the situation you are trying to improve, or whether they concern an older or separate situation. A resentment is nothing but a tightly held set of thoughts and beliefs, and anything that is tightly held on to can bind your energy, and attract negativity into your field. You've probably heard the old saying that "resentment is like taking poison and expecting the other person to die." It's true — resentment poisons your field, and vibrates powerfully out into the quantum field. It sends a set of instructions that attract more of the same circumstances, and it blocks new healthy energy from coming in. So over time, it will be important to clean up any resentments you are carrying. And don't worry if you are having trouble getting excited about the idea. You can use your intention process to affirm that you want to feel more open to the idea. A powerful prayer and affirmation that I learned years ago is this: "I'm willing to be made willing." I have used this prayer and affirmation when I feel resistance within myself. After I tune in to the Universe and express gratitude, I begin my intentions by stating "I intend to release my resentment about such-and-such, and I'm willing to be made willing to do so." I just reaffirm it each day and gradually I feel my heart softening about a troublesome situation or person, and I find myself looking at things from a whole new perspective.

There is another strategy that I have taught my clients, with very exciting results. Let's use the example of cousin Jane for a minute.

Let's say you were counting on Jane to look after your kids for a week, and now that she has pneumonia, she can't. You may resent Jane's doctor for misdiagnosing her several weeks ago, and resent the effort you have to expend to find another caregiver. This resentment can really get in the way of your intention for Jane to get well or for you to get another caregiver. A smart strategy is to tune in to the universe and express gratitude for other things, then start out your intention process by picturing Jane's doctor off to the side or at a distance from the situation. Place the doctor in a bubble of white light. Next, send your best energy into that bubble. State that the doctor's energy (past, present or future) is safely contained within the bubble, and affirm that only his or her positive energy can affect Jane or anyone else. It is quite important that you send the best energy you can towards that bubble. One easy way to do so is to send positive energy from your Highest Self to the doctor's Highest Self. This frees you from the level of earthbound personalities, and allows you to see the doctor as having a wiser, loving self that may not have been evident earlier. This process neutralizes *your* negative energies, as well as the doctor's. In a short time, it will seem as though the energy "logjam" starts to break up — suddenly an alternate caregiver shows up for your kids, Jane's recovery speeds up, the doctor makes some reparative gesture.

My clients and I have used this process in relation to a number of difficult people, and it is absolutely amazing how positively those difficult people have begun to behave within a short time, sometimes just a few days. A bit later, I'll tell you about how Julie used this process about someone in her work environment, with astonishing results!

Special Strategy 4: Overcoming Doubt

If you are someone who really struggles with doubt in your life, you may be feeling that you're not going to be successful with your intentions and affirmations. Be aware that usually this is because earlier life wounds are in the way. These doubts are what I call a "poverty mentality," or a "scarcity mentality," and the usual reason they're there is that your caregivers didn't know how to trust the Universe. They themselves lacked an "abundance mentality" and so they transmitted to you a fear-based way of living. If you haven't already, you probably need to find a good therapist and get those wounds healed. But whether or not you have already done some good healing, if there is a doubting part of you operating here's how you can use the Six Step process to help:

- Tune into the Universe every day in the way that works best for you. Your doubts may be so strong that you can't even believe that you get tuned in to the Universe. Don't worry about that at all. Just find a focal point or process that you like and do it with the intention that the Universe is somehow hearing you. It is, and it doesn't matter at all that you can't feel it right now.

- Express gratitude for anything you can think of, then express gratitude for your doubts! I'm serious. Everything about you can be used by the Universe to move you forward. Say something like "I am grateful that I have doubts because they mean that I really need to be convinced of a benign and abundant Universe. I am grateful for my doubts because when they are overcome, I will have really tested these ideas about the Universe. I appreciate my doubts because they mean I am a thinking person. My doubts are no different than wondering if a loved one will return home — they simply mean I care about the outcome. I am grateful that my doubts will persist only as long as they need to. And I now affirm that each doubt is over-turned, each doubt is turned on its head and transformed into confidence. I don't need to know how. I picture myself as happy, carefree, relaxed in knowing that the Universe provides. It doesn't matter that I haven't pulled that reality into the here-and-now; it's real to the quantum Universe. I'm grateful for however long it takes to trust abundance, and for whatever things need to happen to undo my doubt. I affirm that somehow, my doubts *are* undone." Do this every day, or several times a day.

- Then, express intentions and affirm possibilities that allow the Universe to change your thinking. For example, each day, say "I now draw to me the powerful ways that the Universe intends to make me strong and confident. Each day, moment by moment, I attract situations, circumstances, people, conversations that amazingly change my way of thinking. I affirm that I am amazed and delighted by how powerful these events are. I don't need to know how they occur."

- Plant seeds by using all your tools from Chapter Three. Just keep doing everything you can to shut down negative thinking and fill up the air space with positive possibilities. You must be doing this to prepare the firmware and software of your brain to recognize and register good things as they arrive. Each time you use the tools from Chapter Three, you help your brain to re-wire so that it can eventually self-generate confident thinking. Each time you use the tools, you are inviting the energy of the quantum field to create shifts in your brain.

- If you catch yourself doing fearful or doubtful thinking, tell the Universe to ignore what you were thinking! You can do this because intention can be expressed from any point in time, and so you can retroactively tell the Universe to disregard some earlier thoughts.

- After you have tuned in to the Universe, expressed gratitude, intended and affirmed the changes you desire, and used your daily thinking tools, be sure to finish by saying "and so it is."

Special Strategy 5: Healing Your Shadow Self

When you are ready, you may reach a point where you wish to rise above some aspects of your character. You may realize that in spite of a stable Brain and Body, a healed History, and a pretty positive inner narrative, there are just some habits or patterns in your life that continue to create problems for you. The famous psychologist Carl Jung introduced the idea of the "shadow" self, the dark side of self that we want to hide from others. The shadow self is deep rooted, primitive and behaves self-defensively, creating all kinds of trouble. It can persist beyond very successful healing of other parts of our lives. Because we tend to feel shame about our "weak" or dark aspects of self, we avoid dealing with those troubling parts of self. In fact, even a therapist who knows us well may never know about these parts of our character, because we consciously or unconsciously hide them. But the clues to the shadow self are there in our interactions in our most intimate relationships and/or in our interactions with the world around us. When we are ready to face, heal and evolve our shadow self, its energies can be channeled in powerful and productive ways.

For many of us, the time arrives when the shadow self must be dealt with, when we want to rise above our own self-defeat and behave consistently in congruence with our highest best self. If you find yourself at this place, you are ready to use your Six Step process to set intentions about yourself and the deeper parts of your character. You are ready to attract circumstances that help you to be the best that you can be, to set yourself up for major long term success in your life. In fact, if you've been paying attention, you've probably been attracting these circumstances for some time. If you are cultivating a relationship with the Universe, your highest self has been attracting the feedback about who you are. You have been attracting the learning conditions, and now you'll start to recognize them for what they are. So for example, you may have begun to notice that you keep ending up in long grocery store line-ups, snarled traffic, and at malfunctioning bank machines. I call these things "the Gift in the Garbage Bag." They are the conditions, which when welcomed for their learning potential, can be your greatest blessing. They have arrived because life is telling you that you need to grow in patience, or that you need to lose the narcissistic belief that you should be served faster than everyone else. When you start to recognize that you need to respond differently to these kinds of conditions, you are facing your deepest self. And the more you "lean into it" the quicker you'll benefit. Congratulations! It takes courage to own what you need to change.

So when you use your daily intention process you may say, for example, "I affirm that I attract to myself all the learning and feedback that I need to help me be a more patient person. I am grateful for the conditions that will teach me patience. I affirm that I *am* a patient person." Picture yourself relaxed and content as you wait in the bank lineup or the grocery lineup. Later, when you really are more patient, go ahead and picture short lineups! By then, you may not need conditions which continue to challenge your patience.

Of course, once started, this process may become an ongoing one. For as you confront aspects of your shadow self, the light tends to shine on related areas that need to evolve. And if those other areas don't become obvious to you, then you can use your intention process to invite awareness of them. As you notice them, use positive language to address them, affirming that you attract the experiences that help you to be more loving, kind, assertive, confident, accepting, generous, open-minded or whatever. Picture yourself behaving the way you want to be. Affirm that the outcome exists in the quantum field and that you are now aligning with that higher self. Validate yourself as you make progress, and be patient with yourself as you learn. As they say in the Twelve Step programs, life is about "progress, not perfection."

Special Strategy 6: Strengthening Other Spiritual or Meditative Practices

Ramp up your spiritual or meditation practice! Use the Six Quantum Secrets before, after, or in place of whatever rituals you already practice to connect with the divine. For example, you may start your day with a prayer or a series of prayers, or a liturgy (a liturgy is a ritual way of connecting to the divine, with a community, through ritualized prayers, rites or practices.) You might want to do the Six Quantum Secrets process before or after these rituals, or alternate them, because the two forms of practice become synergistic; they reinforce each other's power.

Or, you might like to combine a simple beginners' Reiki technique with the Six Quantum Secrets process. "Reiki" means "Universal Life-force Energy," and the practice of Reiki involves attuning to divine energy, receiving it through one's body, and gently directing it to balance, heal and harmonize one's own body or someone else's. An easy and pleasant way to attune to the Universe and to the Universal Life-force Energy is to do the Gassho Meditation. You can follow it with the other five steps of the Six Quantum Secrets Process.

THE GASSHO MEDITATION

"Gassho" means "prayer position." Simply quiet yourself, sit upright or cross-legged, and place your palms together, fingers pointing upwards. Concentrate gently on breathing in and out slowly. With each in breath, imagine that Universal Life-force Energy or Light is entering your crown and filling your entire body. Let it swirl through your chakras. Your chakras are seven energy centers in your body, ranging from the base of your spinal cord, and on up through your pelvic/reproductive/sexual area, to your navel, your heart, your throat and neck, your pineal gland or "third eye," to the top of your head. Or just think of the Energy or Light gently streaming down through your crown and through your whole body. With each out breath, visualize that you are exhaling Universal Life-force Energy or Light from every pore in your body and off into infinity. Do this for 10 to 15 minutes. That's all.

Do this as often as you like. And feel free to draw Energy or Light into specific areas of your body that may need healing, picturing it bathing your cells with wholeness.

An easy way to do this is: as the Energy or Light pours through your hands, place your hands gently over any area on your body that requires special attention, and send the Energy or Light into that area.

Feel the unconditional acceptance, connection, and love that the Universe has for you. Just enjoy it and feel gratitude. As you do, you are ready to move on with the remainder of the Six Step Process.

Special Strategy 7: Group Intentions

At any time, and for any reason, you may wish to enlist the assistance of a friend, a group of friends, or a community to which you belong, to create an outcome. This is a particularly great idea if you struggle with doubt, as we talked about above, or if you need healing and perhaps feel too sick or weak to do much on your own. And group intention is especially powerful to accomplish big things in a community or on the planet. Around the world, people have done this to bring peace to a politically troubled area, or to mobilize healing energies to a natural disaster zone. Religious and spiritual communities have used group prayer or meditation to effect global outcomes. Lynne McTaggart, the British author and thinker, regularly conducts group intention experiments via her website and blog.[19] She has led scientifically structured experiments, enlisting people around the world to join together and focus intention. Together her participants have directed their intention, in carefully orchestrated unison, to facilitate physical healing in specific people, and to bring about improvements in water quality, to name just a couple of examples.

One of the great things about group intention is that it can be used in these highly focused ways, when the subject of intention is aware, or it can be used more loosely and informally when the subject or object of intention has no idea whatsoever.

One of my favorite examples of group intention being informally initiated, without the subject's conscious awareness, is reflected in Jim's story. It is also a story of how group intention can re-kindle someone's individual intention, and create miracles:

---

19 Lynne McTaggart, *http://www.theintentionexperiement.com/* (accessed July 31, 2009), and livingthefield.ning.com/profiles/blog/list?user=LynneMcTaggart (accessed July 31, 2009).

Burn Survivor: Jim's Story

Jim, 34, was already a survivor — before the accident. He had worked hard to overcome drug and anger issues, complete his training to become a master welder, and start his own company. And now, with some of those struggles behind him, he was an average working guy trying to make a living and find a little time left over to spend with his fiancée Diane and their four kids.

It was an ordinary work day. Just a few more things to get done before he could call it a day. Someone asked for a quick favor, and Jim, always conscientious and always big-hearted, asked the right questions to make sure that all the fluids were emptied out of a piece of industrial equipment that someone needed welded. Assured that the equipment could be safely worked on, Jim fired up his welding torch and approached the job. Pow!! In the blink of an eye, an inferno exploded, setting Jim on fire. Later Jim would find out that the heat of the fire was so severe that the equipment melted. He knows, from the pattern of his burns, that he must have instinctively started to turn away and shield his eyes. And he remembers the hissing sound of the fire extinguisher as the site boss screamed "get down!" Co-workers surrounded Jim, attempting to smother the flames. A short time later, an ambulance arrived to transport him to hospital.

Mercifully, he doesn't remember much of what happened next. After a severe burn victim arrives at hospital, he is placed in a drug-induced coma. Without consciousness, without struggle, his body would have the best shot at healing. He would not have to remember the torture of having dressings changed, or the torment of waning pain medication. Neither, though, would he be able to communicate to his loved ones that he would survive, that he would be okay.

Jim's fiancée rushed to the hospital, and remembers what it was like to see him, charred. She remembers later, when she went to the accident site, seeing his gloves on the ground and thinking "they're a sign of life, he survived." She did not know, however, what kind of a life Jim would have when he came out of the coma.

Jim was known by everyone as a man of powerful intention. When he set his mind to a task, there was no deterring him from completing it. He was like a bulldog; when he said something would get done, it got done. But here he was, in a coma, hanging between life and death, his conscious self completely unable to exercise intention or affirm his healing. He had second and third degree burns to his head and face, to his neck, arm, hand, back and thigh.

A year before, Diane had started learning about the Law of Attraction, and about the power of intention. So, when her world looked like it was about to fall apart, she did the only thing she could do: on the way to the hospital she had phoned the people closest to her and Jim and asked them to pray or meditate or send their energy to him in the hospital. She later phoned the rest of their family and friends and asked that people send loving intention to help Jim's burns heal. She asked that people send powerful intention to help him with the pain he would experience after he was out of the coma.

And for 22 days, as he lay suspended in a coma, she sat at his bedside, sending healing intention and love into his wounded body.

When Jim was brought out of the coma, the doctors told Diane that Jim would have a long struggle, starting with plastic surgery. They would try to reconstruct the skin on his head and face so that he could face himself in the mirror. They would attempt to build an ear to match the one that was gone. They would try to reconstruct the skin on his hand so that he could have some semblance of mobility.

When the surgeries were over, he would have a battle against mind-numbing pain, and then later physiotherapy which would bring a pain all its own as it stretched his new skin. He would be lucky if he regained mobility. The doctors said that he would be in hospital for two to three months, and that it would be a year before he could contemplate working. His life would be very different, and he would have to earn his living differently. But this sounded like good news compared to death!

And still Diane and her friends and family focused their intention on Jim's healing. In a short time, the medical staff declared that Jim seemed to be defying some odds, seemed to be responding to treatment at a remarkable rate. Soon Jim became alert enough to focus his own intention, and more wonderful things happened. He could move his fingers! He could wear pressure garments that would keep his swelling under control. He became restless, wanted to get up, to move around. And then, true to form, Jim's intention was to leapfrog over all the odds. He wanted to try going without narcotics, he started asking when he could exercise so that he could go back to work! The medical staff shook their heads, and warned him to slow down. In their experience, burn victims didn't rush out of the hospital to go to the gym or return to the site of their life's biggest trauma. But Jim knew from experience what his intention was capable of producing, and Jim's friends and family were happy to add their intentions to support his audacious agenda.

So a couple of months ahead of schedule, defying the odds, Jim was healed enough to go home. He did some physiotherapy, read some books, and got bored. He came in to therapy to work on his feelings about the accident, and about the financial implications of it. He worked through some anger and depression. And three months after third degree burns to a large portion of his body, fuelled by some new vitamins and a lot of intention, Jim went for a hike. He hiked 10 km (that's about 6 miles.)

Another month and he weaned himself off his meds, all the while scheming about ways to go back to work. And almost six months to the day after he was burned, Jim had recovered almost total mobility, his skin grafts and reconstructions had healed beautifully, he'd regained all his weight, rebuilt his muscle mass, and was off sleeping pills. Half a year ahead of his predicted recovery, Jim went back to work. As a welder!

The intention of a loving and determined group of friends and family had gone out into the quantum field and brought home Jim's future. Their collective intention had borne Jim up when he could not consciously set his own intention, and had supported him once he could.

Jim had only one remaining piece of business to take care of. He and Diane set their wedding date for the spring. And no doubt, on that day and in the years that follow, they'll be surrounded by the loving intention of their friends and family for the happy life that already exists for them in the quantum field.

Well, it's time to catch up with Julie and hear how the Six Quantum Secrets brought her dreams into reality. When we last left her, Julie had learned to pay attention to the needs of her Brain and Body, had healed substantial parts of her History, had learned to listen in on her self-talk, and had learned to correct negative self-talk. She had realized that intervening with her inner narrative empowered her over depressed feelings and corrected the negative energy that she vibrated. And she had learned that she needed to continue to do so in order to hear her Inner Voice. She could then send out positive instructions to the quantum field. So let's take a look at how she sent out her intentions, and what she got back!

Julie's Dreams Come True!

Towards the end of Julie's hard work in therapy she was feeling much more unhooked from the past, more able to manage her mood states, and definitely ready for a different kind of future. But as you may recall, one day towards the end of her healing Julie updated me on some current frustrations and disappointments she was experiencing, and I knew she needed to see these in a larger context of meaning. I knew she needed to learn how to connect to the quantum Universe and use the power of the Six Quantum Secrets to change the conditions of her life.

Julie was working in a setting where she had an on-site senior manager, but her direct supervisor was off-site. The on-site senior manager had a tendency to interfere with Julie's job, and her off-site supervisor was half a step behind in supporting Julie in dealing with it. One week, Julie had laboriously arranged a team meeting on a case, coordinating the schedules of about ten busy off-site professionals in order to get them all in attendance. An e-mail went out to all those invited, and was c.c.'ed to Julie's off-site supervisor and her interfering on-site senior manager. The meeting would be in about three weeks. Back came an e-mail from the senior manager, c.c.'ed to everyone, cancelling the meeting! Julie was furious, and deeply demoralized. Her job felt like much more work than it was worth.

On top of that, Julie had appealed her bankruptcy and had been told that she would still owe many thousands of dollars, and that her wages would be automatically deducted and directed to the Bankruptcy Office for years to come. She still had thousands of dollars of student loans to pay on top of that, and owed her parents money. She was also still living in the basement apartment, and had discovered that her landlord was entering her apartment during the day when she was out. In the midst of all this stress, Julie was studying for some final exams in her profession, and had some supervised work hours to complete in order to qualify for her license. And last but not least, Julie was also frustrated because there was a nice man she wanted to date but since they worked together, she knew she couldn't go out with him.

That was the day I explained the quantum field to Julie. I told her about her relationship to the Field, and how her current circumstances could be altered by using her thoughts differently. As you will recall, she had already begun to listen in on her negative self-talk and to correct it, but now she was ready to use directed thought, in the form of Intention, to reach into the quantum field and bring forth different job conditions, better finances, better housing, and more fun.

So here is how we set up the Six Quantum Secrets process for Julie:

1. Tune In to the Universe

Julie could envision a beautiful place where she had witnessed a spectacular sunset, and she decided that every evening, she would light a candle in her room, sit quietly, and picture that beautiful sunset. She might also listen to a favorite piece of music called Cello for Relaxation.

2. Express Gratitude

She would be grateful for these things, realize that they were courtesy of the Universe, and realize that as she felt the beauty of them in her body, she was connecting to the infinite Field. She would express her gratitude daily, understanding that her grateful energy would attract more to be grateful for.

3. Set and Affirm Intentions for Others

In order to change things in her work setting, Julie would need to do a visualization focusing on her on-site senior manager. I encouraged her to picture her manager off to the side or at a distance from the work setting, and to surround her with a bubble of white light. I explained that in order to neutralize this woman's negative energies, she needed to send healing light into that bubble or see it flowing into the bubble from Above. I explained that she didn't have to pretend to love this woman, but she did have to wish her well. She had to send her best energy to the woman, and if she couldn't do it from the level of her earthly self then she could send energy from her Higher Self to the woman's Higher Self. That worked for Julie; she could picture the woman in a healing bubble of white light, and she could project energy above and beyond her earthly connection to the woman by beaming it from her Higher Self to the woman's Higher Self. As she did so, she would intend and affirm "I now affirm that only Sally's best and highest energies may be directed into the work setting and toward my cases. She is safely contained in a bubble of healing light, and only her healthiest energy can be directed outside the bubble. I send my best energy and intention to Sally, and I am grateful for a great outcome at work. I don't have to know what that looks like exactly, but I see my work setting peaceful and functional."

Julie would also use the process to set intention for her roommate, who could be challenging. She put her roommate in a bubble of white light, saying "I now affirm that Jody heals and settles and that we grow close and comfortable as roommates. I affirm a peaceful energy in our home and I am grateful." She sent warm, loving energy into the picture.

Julie set intentions for a friend, visualizing and saying "I now affirm that Jessica receives love and guidance and support in just the way that she needs it, and that she is growing and learning to attract good things to herself. Thank You!" She again sent warm feeling into the intended outcome.

4. Set and Affirm Intentions for Self

Julie would then, one by one, focus on each of the outcomes she desired for the various challenges she was facing. Since she had asked for a review of her bankruptcy appeal, I suggested she focus on an image of the adjudicator at the Bankruptcy Office reviewing her file. I encouraged her to see this person having a sense of compassion and justice, and to set her intention by saying "I now affirm that the person who reviews my bankruptcy file is directed to a decision that is fair and just and in my highest best interest. I am grateful that this person does their job with integrity and balance. I affirm the perfect outcome, and I am grateful."

Then she would picture herself finding the ideal new apartment, run by a good landlord, roomy and in great condition, for an affordable rent. She pictured herself walking out of the apartment, smiling. She affirmed "I now find the perfect apartment, in a great location, with a good landlord, and I am grateful. It exists in the quantum realm, and it exists here in my city, and I am directed to it with ease."

Julie also intended and affirmed that she would do well on her exams, have all the support she needed in her work setting to complete her supervised hours, and qualify for her license with ease. She pictured these outcomes, sent warm energy into the pictures, and affirmed the outcomes with gratitude.

She knew that her long-term intentions would also include clearing her student loans, dating a nice man and having more fun, but for the first few weeks of her Six Step Process she would just concentrate on her short and medium term intentions.

5. *Plant the Seeds of Change*

Julie knew she needed to plant seeds to support her intentions, and so she determined that she would look at apartment listings and go out to see apartments as soon as possible. She got it that she would hold on to her vision of what she wanted, but would be somewhat flexible about what she looked at in order to give the Universe multiple avenues to express itself.

She knew that she would support her intentions about her career by studying hard and taking whatever steps necessary to arrange on-site supervision as soon as she passed her exams.

And she knew that she would plant seeds later for her longer-term intentions by seeking a job with a higher income, by refining her processes of looking for a man, and by expanding her ways of interacting with the world.

6. *Affirm that Intentions are Accomplished*

Julie would gratefully affirm the outcome at the end of each individual visualization and intention, and at the end of practicing the Six Quantum Secrets each day she would also say "And so it is." She also really liked an image from Dr. Wayne Dyer's *The Power of Intention,*[20] in which he envisioned himself holding onto a trolley strap as a streetcar took him wherever he wanted to go.

So when Julie would say "and so it is," she would picture herself reaching up and holding on to a trolley strap and going wherever she wanted to go.

For the next two weeks, all we wanted Julie to do was enjoy using her Six Quantum Secrets every day. Julie implemented the process faithfully. On the 16th day she arrived for her appointment, looking amazed, and said to me "You're not going to believe it! I don't even know where to start!" This is what Julie reported:

---

20 Dyer, W. (2004.) *The Power of Intention*. Carlsbad, California: Hay House Inc.

"First I got a call from the Bankruptcy office, cutting two months off my repayment schedule, but last week they called me again and reduced my entire bankruptcy to $1300 payable over the next few months and I will be cleared from bankruptcy, years earlier than I was supposed to be! Then I got an e-mail from my off-site supervisor saying she was advising everyone that the team meeting I had set would go ahead! And then the interfering senior manager e-mailed me saying she hoped I'd had a nice break over the holidays and that since the team meeting was apparently going ahead, she looked forward to seeing me there and to working with me in the months ahead! Then someone at work came to me and said they knew I wasn't too happy at our office, and that they had heard of a great job I should apply for, so I applied and I have an interview! Then out of the blue, the woman who used to be married to my ex tracked me down from thousands of miles away and sent me an e-mail to apologize for being so mean to me when I was with her ex-husband! Then I decided to go and see if there were any vacant apartments at a nice building I used to live at. The building manager recognized me, I told him I was just coming out of bankruptcy and that it might affect my credit rating when he checked on me, and he said "that's ok, I appreciate your honesty. You were a good tenant, and I'd be happy to rent to you. I hope it's a 2 bedroom that you and your roommate want, because I just had an unusually large one become available and I can show it to you today." It was perfect, fit my budget, and we move in in less than a month!"

Julie paused for breath, and then she rolled her eyes heavenward as she said, "I'm saving the most surprising for last. You won't believe this. A few months ago a group of my girlfriends planned a trip to a luxury resort. It's a junket, so they pre-paid the airfare and all the costs. Yesterday one of my girlfriends called me and said she can't go and she wants me to have her ticket!

So I move into my great new apartment in three weeks, will be close to being cleared from bankruptcy, got the support I needed at work, got an apology from someone out of the blue from thousands of miles away, and to celebrate it all I get to go to a luxury resort, all expenses paid, one week after I move into my new apartment!" And this was just 16 days after Julie began practicing the Six Quantum Secrets!

So Julie was on a roll, and she kept at it, using her meditation, gratitude, intention and affirmation processes every day. She began to specifically affirm regarding the supervised hours she needed to fulfill her license requirements. She'd say," I now affirm that I draw to me the perfect or ideal situation to comfortably complete my supervised hours, with pay, with an ideal supervisor." Three weeks later, Julie had been offered the great new job that she had interviewed for. And they so wanted her that they offered to arrange special supervision so that she could complete the requirements for her license, at no cost to her! With the boosted confidence she felt from her intention successes, and knowing that she would be leaving her current job, she decided to risk letting her really nice male co-worker know that she would like to spend more time with him. So he asked her out!

Everyone who knew Julie said, "what are you doing?! How come your whole life has changed? And so suddenly! You're not even living the same life you were living a couple of months ago!"

Julie just kept on having fun with the Six Quantum Secrets. Just before she was to move out of her old apartment, she and her roommate needed a new vacuum, so that they could leave their old place immaculate. Julie briefly affirmed an intention for a new vacuum and within 24 hours someone phoned her roommate and offered her a new vacuum!

And so in the following months, Julie and I worked on affirmations to use with some of her medium-term and long-term intentions. These are the affirmations she chose to use:

- "I affirm that I feel well-rested, study easily with great concentration, intuitively sense that I am mastering the material, and confidently prepare and pass the licensing exam."
- "I now affirm that I am drawing to myself all the ideas and inspiration and perspective to know exactly how to handle whatever challenges come up for me. I grow wiser and calmer, and I *am* wise and calm."
- "I affirm that I now create the conditions for a loving partnership with a mature, responsible man with whom I will share a life of integrity and passion."
- "I affirm that I am drawing to me all the guidance and wisdom I need to maintain my balance, my equilibrium, to make healthy choices and to rise to my highest potential."

Six months later, Julie and I reviewed how far she had come in her life. She had paid off her bankruptcy balance, and had almost completed her licensing requirements. Her benefits at work would kick in shortly and pay all fees related to her exams and license. She had started yoga as a way to take care of her Brain and Body. After dating her former co-worker for a while, she realized he was not emotionally available, and so she exercised new wisdom and maturity to end the relationship. She had begun to look in more fertile places for suitable men, and was attracting men better suited to her. She said "I have learned to turn away men who show the slightest sign of disrespect. I am learning not to be too available." She had realized that her own history and biology could leave her vulnerable to dysthymia and depressive states, but that "I can now pull myself out of depression. I get it that I can have one bad thing going on in my life and it doesn't have to affect the other parts of my life."

When I looked back on Julie's journey, I felt proud and privileged to have watched her transformation. She demonstrated the power of connecting to the quantum field, the power of gratitude, of intention, and of affirmation. She had affirmed that she would draw to herself all the guidance and wisdom she needed to maintain her balance and her equilibrium to make healthy choices. She had done so. And best of all, she was now living out the most powerful and eloquent part of her affirmation: "I will rise to my highest potential."

If You're Still Stuck …

With a healthy Brain and Body, a healed History, and the clarity of mind to hear your Inner Voice, you should be feeling and enjoying your connection to the quantum Universe. But if you are not yet fully healed in the first Three Domains, you may not yet have the connection to the energies of the quantum Field that you desire. Not to worry! Pursue healing in the Three Domains as best you can. As you do, go ahead and start using the Six Quantum Secrets. Here's how you can do that:

1. Tell the Universe that you want a connection. Do this every day. It takes you seriously. If you have doubts or anger, tell the Universe you do, but do not blame the Universe for what's wrong. You have been a co-creator of your life for a very long time and fixing it will mean opening yourself to a cooperative relationship with the Universe, not a blaming one. Tell the Universe that you are open to losing your anger, fear and doubt, and mean it.

2. If you do not have the healing resources available that you need for Brain and Body, tell the Universe that you intend to attract them, and affirm that those resources exist somewhere and your desire to find them naturally draws them to you.

Plant seeds by affirming this every day and diligently looking for the resources you need, with whatever conditions you need (low-cost, local, insurable, or whatever.)

3. Affirm that other resources beyond your imagining are aligning for you, and stay open. Watch for little clues (the "trail of breadcrumbs.")

4. Practice gratitude every day for *something*. This is essential to keep you connected to the resources of the quantum field.

5. Create a picture in your head of your healed life, and re-run it many times a day. Energy flows where attention goes, so your picture of a healed life is a beacon or magnet that attracts the energies that make it possible.

6. Ask other healthy happy people to hold you in their consciousness, their prayers, their meditation — however it works best for them. Ask them what you can do for them in return. Use the inter-connectedness of the quantum field in this way to keep generative energy working.

7. If you do not give up, the Universe will show up for you. It is physically incapable of doing anything else. Don't get hung up on the time frame — ice doesn't break up til the spring, chicks don't break out of their shells til they're ready, plants don't grow til they've been in the ground a while. All of nature instructs us that we are in a *process*. In the western world, we tend to be pretty impatient about most things — the drive-thru is too slow, the microwave isn't fast enough, we don't even like the wait for the kettle to boil. You'll have to let go of your impatience, because when you say "it's too slow," the Universe says "yes, we can do slow." And the Universe often acts in paradox — when you let go of urgency, it delivers. As soon as you get the lesson it's over!

8. Know that the loving intention behind this book is with you, crossing time and space. You are not alone.

———⌣———

And so we come full circle, back to the Great Pyramid. Your healthy Brain and Body, your healed History, the clarity of mind to hear your Inner Voice together create a structure for your life. They support you to rise up to a peak, to connect to the Universe, to reflect your beauty to the world and to radiate energy that makes your highest dreams come true.

The Six Quantum Secrets to an Amazing Life form a set of blueprints. So begin. Let your dreams inspire the design of your own life. Tune In to the Universe to lay the foundation that will support everything. Express Gratitude; it's the mortar that holds everything together. Through your Intentions and Affirmations, offer a design for the Universe to work with. Plant Seeds of Change and Affirm the outcome. Through the miraculous alchemy of the quantum field, *your energies transform into the material.* Your vision is made manifest, your life rises up to a peak. Your beauty is visible to the world. Go Live your Dream.

Appendix

RESOURCES and LINKS

Supports to Heal and to Manifest your Dreams

"May the road rise up to meet you,
May the wind always be at your back,
May the sun shine warm upon your face,
the rains fall soft upon your fields ...
A traditional Gaelic invocation of abundance

A NOTE TO THE READER

The following resources are for information only. Maureen Kitchur does not endorse specific organizations, practitioners or practices. It is recommended that consumers educate themselves about any treatment method or practitioner listed in this Appendix, and consult with their family physician before selecting treatment resources.

ALCOHOL ADDICTION:

- Alcoholics Anonymous: www.aa.org   Go on-line to look for a 12 Step meeting, or look in your local phone directory.

- AA is also associated with Al-Anon, for family members of the alcohol-dependent: www.al-anon.alateen.org

Look for other Al-Anon weblinks in your part of the world, and check your phone directory.

COCAINE ADDICTION:

www.ca.org

NARCOTICS ADDICTION:

www.na.org

If you can't find a CA or NA group near you, you'll be very welcome at AA.

FOOD ADDICTION:

Overeaters Anonymous at www.oa.org

For international meeting times of addictions groups:
http://www.aa.ca/setcountry/

SEXUAL ADDICTION:

First check out the website for the Society for the Advancement of Sexual Health, where you can get educated: www.sash.net. You can also take a self-test on-line to see if you have a problem.

Then look for 12 Step support groups such as:

- Sexaholics Anonymous (SA):   www.sa.org
- Sex Addicts Anonymous (SAA):   www.saa-recovery.org
- Sex and Love Addicts Anonymous (SLAA):   www.slaafws.org
- S-Anon for family members of sex addicts: www.sanon.org

For qualified therapists to help with sexual addiction, go to: www.iitap.com

For qualified therapists to help with illegal sexual behaviors, go to: www.atsa.com

GAMBLING ADDICTION:

For 12 Step Meetings, look for Gamblers Anonymous:

- in the U.S.:   www.gamblersanonymous.org
- in Canada: www.gamblersanonymous.ca

ADRENAL FATIGUE/ADRENAL BURNOUT:

- To check out whether some of your Brain and Body problems, including possible chronic fatigue and fibromyalgia, are related to depleted adrenal glands, go to www.adrenalfatigue.org
- Since chronic fatigue and fibromyalgia can be confused with, or exacerbated by thyroid problems and depleted adrenal glands, consider having your health care professional order urinary thyroid testing and/or testing of adrenal hormones. For more information, check the website of Rocky Mountain

Laboratories at www.rmalab.com or www.salivatest.com or check the website of ZRT Laboratories at www.zrtlab.com

ATTENTION DEFICIT DISORDER, ATTENTION DEFICIT HYPERACTIVE DISORDER, AND ANXIETY & DEPRESSION:

- Dr. Daniel Amen has authored several reader-friendly books on brain disorders, and in them he provides guidelines for nutritional supplements and medications.

  - Look for: *Healing ADD: The Breakthrough Program.* New York: Berkley Books, 2001.

  - *Healing Anxiety and Depression.* New York: Putnam, 2003.

  - *Healing the Hardware of the Soul.* New York: Free Press, 2002

- Dr. Amen also has a great website, and a free newsletter, available at www.amenclinics.com where you can also take on-line tests for ADD and ADHD.

BORDERLINE PERSONALITY DISORDER:

- Borderline personality disorder is treated with Dialectical Behavior Therapy (DBT). For information about both, check out the U.S. National Institute of Mental Health at http://www.nimh.nih.gov/health/publications/borderline-personality-disorder-fact-sheet/index.shtml.

- In Canada: www.borderlinepersonality.ca

- Two excellent books:

  - *Sometimes I Act Crazy: Living with Borderline Personality* by Jerold Kreisman, M.D. and Hal Straus. New Jersey: John Wiley & Sons, 2004.

  - *Stop Walking on Eggshells: Taking Your Life Back when Someone You Care About Has Borderline Personality Disorder* by Paul Mason and Randi Kreger. Oakland, CA: New Harbinger Publications, Inc., 1998.

FUNCTIONAL MEDICINE:

- For medical care that takes account of the whole person, check out the Institute for Functional Medicine at: www.functionalmedicine.org

HORMONES, SALIVA TESTING, ALLERGY TESTING AND BIO-IDENTICAL HORMONE REPLACEMENT:

Rocky Mountain Analytical Laboratories:

- for information about hormones, hormone testing and other preventive medicine tests in Canada go to www.rmalab.com

- for information about menopause and bio-identical hormone replacement, Rocky Mountain Labs carries the book *You've Hit Menopause: Now What?* by Dr. George Gillson and Tracy Marsden, B.Sc. Pharm. The book is also available at www.amazon.com

ZRT Laboratories:

- for information about hormones, hormone testing and hormone replacement go to: www.salivatest.com and www.zrtlab.com

PROTEIN, ESSENTIAL FATTY ACID AND NUTRITION GUIDELINES:

- *Health Canada recommendations:* www.hc-sc.gc.ca/fn-an/ nutrition/reference/table/ref_macronutr_tbl-eng.php

- *Health Canada — Canada's Food Guide:* www.hc-sc.gc.ca/fn-an/food-guide-aliment/basics-base/serving-portion-eng.php

- *The United States Department of Agriculture — Food and Nutrition Information Centre:* http://fnic.nal.usda.gov/

- *USDA Dietary Guidelines for Americans:* www.health.gov/dietaryguidelines

Psychotherapy and Counseling:

For information about effective healing methods check the websites of the following organizations. Most of them also have directories or links on their sites to help you find a clinician in your area:

- *American Association of Marriage and Family Therapists (AAMFT):* www.aamft.org

- *American Medical Association:* www.ama-assn.org

- *American Psychological Association:* www.apa.org

- *American Society for Clinical Hypnosis:* www.asch.net

- *The EMDR Institute:* www.emdr.com

- *National Association of Cognitive-Behavioral Therapists:* www.nacbt.org

- *Imago Couple Therapy:* www.gettingtheloveyouwant.com

Alternative and Complementary Therapies:

Alternative and complementary healing practices can be a good adjunct to counseling or psychotherapy. For information about well-established methods:

- *Craniosacral Therapy:* The Upledger Institute at www.upledger.com or The Biodynamic Craniosacral Therapy Association of North America at www.craniosacraltherapy.org

- *Healing Touch:* Healing Touch Canada is a Certified Canadian Educational Institution that teaches an energy based approach to health and healing. For information and a list of practitioners: www.healingtouchcanada.net

- *Accupressure:* Acupressure is a traditional Chinese medicine (TCM) technique derived from acupuncture (a blend of "acupuncture" and "pressure.") www.accupressure.com

- *Emotional Freedom Techniques (EFT):* EFT is a needle-free version of acupuncture that works with the body's energy systems to facilitate emotional healing: www.emofree.com

- *Chi Gong (or Qigong):* Learn about the ancient Chinese healing practice at www.chigong.com

INDEX

"n" refers to notes.